CGP — books like no others!

CGP

GCSE English Literature AQA Anthology

The Study Guide

Poems from
Duffy, Armitage, pre-1914

AQA A Specification — Higher Level

This book is a step-by-step guide to becoming an expert on the Anthology part of your GCSE English Literature exam.

It's got everything you need to know — annotated poems, exam themes and worked essays.

It's ideal for use as a classroom study book or a revision guide.

CONTENTS

Section Four — Themes: Ideas, Attitudes and Feelings

Section Five — Themes: Methods of Poetry

Section Six — How to Answer the Question

☆ = Key poems as suggested by AQA

Published by Coordination Group Publications Ltd.

Editors:
Charley Darbishire, Kate Houghton, Kate Redmond, Katherine Reed, Edward Robinson.

Contributors:
Margaret Giordmaine, Roland Haynes, Shelagh Moore, Elisabeth Sanderson, Nicola Woodfin.

With thanks to Kate Houghton, Jennifer Underwood and Paula Barnett for the proofreading.

ISBN-10: 1 84146 354 X
ISBN-13: 978 1 84146 354 4
Groovy website: www.cgpbooks.co.uk
Jolly bits of clipart from CorelDRAW®
Printed by Elanders Hindson Ltd, Newcastle upon Tyne.

How To Use This Book

This book will help you to do better in your GCSE English Literature Anthology Exam. It's full of straightforward ways of getting extra marks. Start by asking your teacher which poems and themes you need to study: some schools get you to study all of them, others pick out certain ones.

There are Six Sections in this book

Sections One, Two and Three are about the Poems

There are two pages about each poem. This is what the pages look like:

There's a nice picture of the poet and some info about their life.

Important or tricky bits of the poem are highlighted and explained.

Difficult words are defined in the poem dictionary.

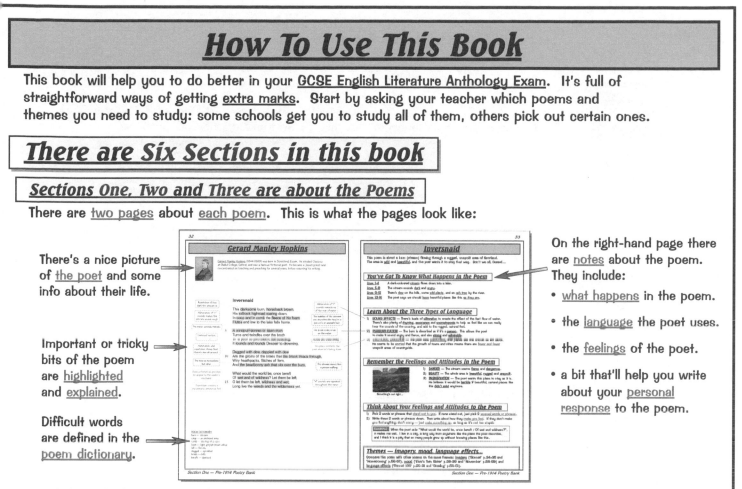

On the right-hand page there are notes about the poem. They include:

• what happens in the poem.
• the language the poet uses.
• the feelings of the poet.
• a bit that'll help you write about your personal response to the poem.

Read through the pages on the poems you've been told to study. When you've read about each poem, shut the book and write out as much as you can remember. See what you've left out, then do it again.

Sections Four and Five are about the Themes

In the exam, you'll have to compare how four poems relate to one of the themes. In Sections Four and Five, there's a page about each of the main themes that might come up. The pages tell you which poems use each theme and how different poets treat the same theme. Read them, understand them and learn them.

Section Six is about Preparing for your Exam

Pages 84-85 tell you how to plan and write good essays using CGP's 5-step method. The section also includes sample exam questions with 'A' grade answers.

Sample exam question.

A sample plan for how you could answer the exam question.

A sample student answer, which continues on the opposite page.

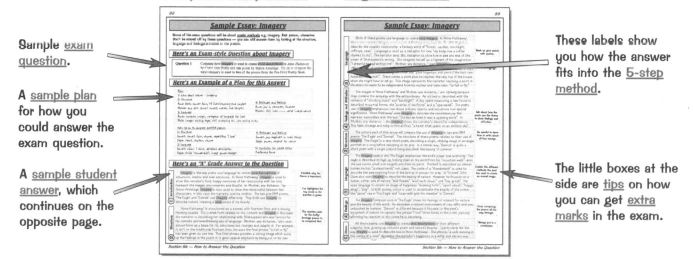

These labels show you how the answer fits into the 5-step method.

The little boxes at the side are tips on how you can get extra marks in the exam.

Write some essays using the 5-step method. Use the exam-style questions in the CGP Duffy and Armitage Anthology Workbook, if you have it, or ask your teacher for some practice questions. You get one hour to answer the question in the exam, so practise doing some timed essays.

Key Poem

Ben Jonson

Ben Jonson (1572-1637) was the son of a clergyman. He attended Westminster School, before becoming a bricklayer and later joining the army. He went on to become one of the most important poets of his time. He also wrote plays and was a friend of William Shakespeare.

The poem is written directly to his son. It's his way of saying a fond goodbye.

His "sinne" was hoping that his son would live for a long time.

Suggests that he thinks that his son's death was inevitable and something he could not control.

Jonson seems to want to be dead too.

Shows his affection for his son.

His son was his greatest creation.

He decides he'll never love anyone else so dearly because he doesn't want to feel so much pain again.

He loved his son very much.

Uses money as a metaphor. Jonson's son was "lent" to him for seven years and now he has to "pay" his debt through the death of his son.

Says there are advantages of being dead, e.g. you don't have to suffer pain and old age.

This type of language is usually found on a gravestone — the poem commemorates Jonson's son.

On my first Sonne

Farewell, thou child of my right hand, and joy;
My sinne was too much hope of thee, lov'd boy,
Seven yeeres tho'wert lent to me, and I thee pay,
Exacted by thy fate, on the just day.
5 O, could I loose all father, now. For why
Will man lament the state he should envie?
To have so soone scap'd worlds, and fleshes rage,
And, if no other miserie, yet age?
Rest in soft peace, and, ask'd, say here doth lye
10 Ben. Jonson his best piece of poetrie.
For whose sake, hence-forth, all his vowes be such,
As what he loves may never like too much.

POEM DICTIONARY
sinne — an old way of spelling sin
yeeres — years
tho'wert — you were
lament — to feel sorrow or regret
scap'd — a shortened way of writing escaped
miserie — an old way of spelling misery
hence-forth — from now on

On my first Sonne

This is a simple poem about a father who is <u>mourning</u> the death of his seven year-old <u>son</u>.
The poem is the father's way of <u>saying goodbye</u> to his son.

You've Got to Know What Happens in the Poem

<u>Lines 1-4</u>   The man says <u>goodbye</u> to his seven year old son who has just <u>died</u>.

<u>Lines 5-8</u>   He says he <u>envies</u> his son because in <u>heaven</u> you don't have to
deal with all the <u>horrible</u> things that happen in life.

<u>Lines 9-12</u>   Ben Jonson says that his <u>son</u> was his best ever <u>creation</u>. He decides that in the future he
won't <u>love</u> anyone as much as he loved his son so that he won't get so <u>upset</u> if they die.

Learn About the Three Types of Language

1) <u>PRIDE and AFFECTION</u> — The poet is very <u>fond</u> of his son. The poem is written as though he's <u>talking directly</u> to him. This makes it seem very <u>personal</u> and helps you to imagine the poet's <u>feelings</u>.

2) <u>METAPHORICAL LANGUAGE</u> — A metaphor about <u>debt</u> and <u>money</u> explains why his son died.

3) <u>COMMENTS ABOUT DEATH</u> — There are quite a few different ideas about <u>death</u> in this poem. On one hand the poet is <u>sad</u> that his son's dead, on the other he says that early death isn't all bad because you don't have to <u>grow old</u> and suffer <u>pain</u>.

Remember the Feelings and Attitudes in the Poem

1) <u>GRIEF</u> — The poet is really <u>upset</u> about the <u>death</u> of his son.

2) <u>UNCERTAINTY</u> — The poet <u>wonders</u> whether it is better to be dead than to be alive.

3) <u>PAIN</u> — He's so <u>devastated</u> by his son's death that he decides never to love anyone else as much, because he doesn't want to <u>suffer</u> like this again.

Think About Your Feelings and Attitudes to the Poem

1) Pick 2 words or phrases that <u>stand out to you</u>. If none stand out, just pick 2 unusual words or phrases.

2) Write these 2 words or phrases down. Then write about how they <u>make you feel</u>. If they don't make you feel anything, don't worry — just <u>make something up</u>, as long as it's <u>not too stupid</u>.

> **EXAMPLE** I find it very touching that the poet describes his son as his "best piece of poetrie". Even though he was one of the best poets of his time, he thinks that having a son was a greater achievement than his writing.

Themes — death, parent/child relationships, love...

You can compare this poem with other poems about the same themes: <u>death</u> ('Tichborne's Elegy' p.14-15), <u>parent/child relationships</u> ('Before You Were Mine' p.44-45, 'Mother, any distance' p.52-53 and 'Kid' p.60-61), and <u>love</u> ('Anne Hathaway' p.40-41).

William Butler Yeats

William Butler Yeats (1865-1939) was born in Dublin. He is often considered to be Ireland's greatest ever poet. As well as poetry, Yeats wrote many plays and won the Nobel Prize for Literature. He was also involved in the Celtic Revival, a movement to encourage traditional Irish culture and discourage English influences on Ireland.

Shows the poem is from the point of view of the old mother.

The old woman gets up really early whilst the young people lie about in bed — this is emphasised by alliteration.

Young people are only concerned by trivial matters.

The woman thinks that young people are always moaning about things that aren't important.

Suggests that the woman has no choice.

The poem is in rhyming couplets.

List of all the rubbish jobs that the old woman has to do.

Slow, plodding rhythm suggests the boring, repetitive tasks.

Use of 'their' and 'I' emphasises the differences between the old woman and the young people.

Fire going out could be a symbol for her life coming to an end.

The Song of the Old Mother

I rise in the dawn, and I kneel and blow
Till the seed of the fire flicker and glow;
And then I must scrub and bake and sweep
Till stars are beginning to blink and peep;
5   And the young lie long and dream in their bed
Of the matching of ribbons for bosom and head,
And their day goes over in idleness,
And they sigh if the wind but lift a tress:
While I must work because I am old,
10 And the seed of the fire gets feeble and cold.

The woman gets the fire going in the morning, but by the end of the day it's going out — she'll have to do it all again the next day. This emphasises how boring and repetitive her life is.

The woman's work makes her tired and weak, just as the fire gets weaker as the day goes on.

POEM DICTIONARY
tress — a lock of hair

The Song of the Old Mother

In this poem an <u>old woman</u> describes the daily <u>chores</u> she has to do. She seems to think that people in younger generations are a bit lazy and that they have a much easier life than she does.

You've Got to Know What Happens in the Poem

<u>Lines 1-2</u>   The old woman gets up and gets the <u>fire</u> going.

<u>Lines 3-4</u>   She does <u>cooking</u> and <u>cleaning</u> until night time.

<u>Lines 5-8</u>   The woman thinks that <u>younger people</u> (possibly her children) are <u>lazy</u> and that they don't have to do as much <u>hard work</u> as she has to.

<u>Line 9-10</u>   The woman summarises her <u>attitude</u> to <u>life</u> and the <u>fire</u> she has made starts to <u>go out</u>.

Learn About the Two Types of Language

1) <u>RHYMING COUPLETS AND RHYTHM</u> — the <u>rhyming couplets</u> make the poem sound <u>repetitive</u> like the woman's <u>work</u>. The <u>regular rhythm</u> also makes the poem read like a <u>song</u> which ties in with the <u>title</u> of the poem.

2) <u>CONTRAST</u> — Yeats points out all the <u>differences</u> between the life that the old woman lives and the lives of the young people using lists and descriptions of their daily <u>activities</u> and <u>thoughts</u>.

Remember the Feelings and Attitudes in the Poem

1) <u>SYMPATHY</u> — The poet <u>feels sorry</u> for the old mother.

2) <u>DRUDGERY</u> — The poet thinks that the woman's life will <u>inevitably</u> carry on like this until she <u>dies</u>.

3) <u>MORAL</u> — Yeats uses the poem to show people what life is like for <u>old people</u> who have to do lots of <u>work</u> — perhaps he hopes that it will <u>change</u> people's attitudes towards poor elderly people.

Think About Your Feelings and Attitudes to the Poem

1) Pick 2 words or phrases that <u>stand out to you</u>. If none stand out, just pick 2 unusual words or phrases.

2) Write these 2 words or phrases down. Then write about how they <u>make you feel</u>. If they don't make you feel anything, don't worry — just <u>make something up</u>, as long as it's <u>not too stupid</u>.

> **EXAMPLE** The phrase "lie long and dream in their bed" makes me feel sympathy for the woman in the poem and anger towards the idle young people. The phrase highlights the stark difference between the lives of the young people and the old woman's life.

Themes — attitudes to others, first person, imagery...

You could compare this poem with other poems about the same themes: <u>attitudes towards other people</u> ('Before You Were Mine' p.44-45 and 'November' p.58-59), <u>use of first person</u> ('The Affliction of Margaret' p.10-11) and <u>imagery</u> ('Homecoming' p.56-57).

THIS IS A FLAP.
FOLD THIS PAGE OUT.

The Affliction of Margaret

The poet describes the feelings of Margaret, a woman whose <u>son</u> has been <u>missing</u> for seven years. She <u>fears the worst</u>, and she's desperate to talk to him.

You've Got to Know What Happens in the Poem

<u>Lines 1-14</u>   Margaret describes the <u>pain</u> of not knowing <u>where her son is</u>.
<u>Lines 15-21</u>   She goes on about how <u>good-looking</u> and <u>well-meaning</u> her son was.
<u>Lines 22-28</u>   She says children <u>don't realise</u> how much their <u>mothers worry</u> about them.
<u>Lines 29-42</u>   Margaret says she was a <u>good mother</u>. She wants her son to <u>return</u>, whatever state he's in.
<u>Lines 43-49</u>   She says that <u>birds</u> have wings, so they're <u>free</u> to return. People <u>don't have</u> this freedom.
<u>Lines 50-56</u>   She imagines terrible things happening to her son, like being <u>imprisoned</u> or <u>shipwrecked</u>.
<u>Lines 57-70</u>   She says it's <u>impossible</u> to talk to the <u>dead</u>. There's <u>no escape</u> from her fears.
<u>Lines 71-77</u>   <u>No-one</u> can understand her grief. Her son <u>returning</u> to her is the only way to end it.

Learn About the Three Types of Language

1) <u>OBSESSIVE LANGUAGE</u> — Thoughts of Margaret's son have completely <u>taken over</u> her life. Her thoughts are <u>illogical</u>, and she feels she <u>can't be happy</u> about anything while her son's still missing.

2) <u>PAIN and FEAR</u> — She seems to <u>torture herself</u> by thinking of all the <u>awful things</u> that might have happened to him. She feels that it would be better to know he was dead than not to know anything.

3) <u>REFLECTIVE LANGUAGE</u> — She's sometimes more <u>reasoning</u>, trying to find answers. She feels she <u>can't explain</u> her feelings to anyone — she's <u>alone</u> with her sorrow, and desperate just to <u>talk</u> to her son.

Remember the Feelings and Attitudes in the Poem

"I hope he's got some clean underpants..."

1) <u>SYMPATHY</u> — The poet <u>feels sorry</u> for Margaret.
2) <u>ANXIETY</u> — He shows how <u>anxious</u> she is to find out how her son is.
3) <u>DESPERATION</u> — She feels absolutely <u>desperate</u> — nothing matters to her but her son.

Margaret's quite <u>irrational</u> at times — she tries to talk to him even though he's not there, and her mind jumps from one thought to another fairly randomly.

Think About Your Feelings and Attitudes to the Poem

1) Pick 2 words or phrases that <u>stand out to you</u>. If none stand out, just pick 2 <u>unusual words or phrases</u>.
2) Write these 2 words or phrases down. Then write about how they <u>make you feel</u>. If they don't make you feel anything, don't worry — just <u>make something up</u>, as long as it's not too stupid.

EXAMPLE The phrase "I've wet my path with tears like dew" makes me feel great sorrow for the mother. It seems there is no end to her suffering, and her pain follows her wherever she goes.

Themes — parent/child relationships, strong emotions...

You could compare 'The Affliction of Margaret' with other poems about the same themes: <u>parent/child relationships</u> ('On my first Sonne' p.6-7 and 'Mother, any distance' p.52-53) and <u>strong emotions</u> ('Havisham' p.36-37 and 'Kid' p.60-61).

William Blake

<u>William Blake</u> (1757-1827) was born in London and educated at home by his mother. He was a poet, artist, engraver and publisher. He believed in the power of the imagination and religion over materialism.

The lost child could be a metaphor for someone who's lost their faith.

The Little Boy Lost

The boy calls after his dad, but "father" could also mean God.

He's lost and can't see his way without God to guide him.

'Father, father, where are you going?
Oh do not walk so fast!
Speak, father, speak to your little boy
Or else I shall be lost.'

The boy sounds desperate and helpless.

The child seems doomed on his own.

5   The night was dark, no father was there,
The child was wet with dew;
The mire was deep, and the child did weep,
And away the vapour flew.

Could be some kind of guiding light or spirit.

As well as being found, this could mean someone who's found their faith again.

The Little Boy Found

This can be interpreted in different ways. The light could be like the star that led the wise men to the baby Jesus. Or it could be a bad spirit that is leading the little boy into danger.

The little boy lost in the lonely fen,
Led by the wand'ring light,
Began to cry; but God, ever nigh,
Appeared like his father in white.

Suggests God is always there for you when you need him.

God is a much better father to the boy than his actual father.

The boy's mum seems devoted and loving — unlike his dad who failed to look after him.

5   He kissed the child, and by the hand led,
And to his mother brought,
Who in sorrow pale, through the lonely dale
Her little boy weeping sought.

God shows the boy the way home — compare this with line 5 above.

The mother has been crying, just like the boy.

POEM DICTIONARY
mire — mud
fen — a marshy area
nigh — near
dale — a valley in a hilly area

The Little Boy Lost and The Little Boy Found

These two poems go together to tell a sweet little tale about a little boy who gets lost...
and then gets found again, with a bit of help from God. The poems have a <u>religious message</u>
— the poet says that God will show us the way when we're lost.

You've Got to Know What Happens in the Poems

The Little Boy Lost

Lines 1-4   A little boy calls out to his <u>dad</u>, asking him to wait so he doesn't get <u>lost</u>.

Lines 5-8   But his dad disappears, leaving the boy <u>lost</u> and <u>crying</u> in the rain.

The Little Boy Found

Lines 1-4   The boy's <u>lost</u> on his own, but luckily for him <u>God</u> shows up.

Lines 5-8   God leads the boy back to his <u>mum</u>, who was out <u>looking for him</u>.

Learn About the Two Types of Language

1) **EMOTIVE LANGUAGE** — The poet's descriptions of the boy make him seem <u>helpless</u> and <u>vulnerable</u>. This makes the reader <u>pity him</u>. It also shows how he <u>can't cope</u> on his own.

2) **RELIGIOUS LANGUAGE** — There's lots of <u>Christian imagery</u> in the poem. This supports the overall <u>religious message</u> — that we are <u>lost without God</u>, and can only find safety with his help.

Remember the Feelings and Attitudes in the Poems

These two poems are a bit boring, so here's a picture of something more exciting.

1) <u>FEAR</u> — The boy is <u>desperate</u> and <u>scared</u>.

2) <u>CONCERN</u> — His mother is <u>worried sick</u> about her son.

3) <u>RELIGION</u> — The poet believes people are only <u>safe</u> when they're with <u>God</u>. He thinks people are <u>lost without God</u>.

Think About Your Feelings and Attitudes to the Poems

1) Pick 2 words or phrases that <u>stand out to you</u>. If none stand out, just pick 2 <u>unusual words or phrases</u>.

2) Write these 2 words or phrases down. Then write about how they <u>make you feel</u>. If they don't make you feel anything, don't worry — just <u>make something up</u>, as long as it's not too stupid.

> **EXAMPLE** When the child says "Speak, father, speak to your little boy", I feel really sorry for him. He seems completely helpless and unable to survive on his own.

Themes — danger, strong emotions, imagery...

Compare this poem with other poems on the same themes: <u>danger</u> ('Stealing' p.50-51 and 'Hitcher' p.66-67), <u>strong emotions</u> ('The Affliction of Margaret' p.10-11 and 'My father thought it bloody queer' p.54-55) and <u>imagery</u> ('Havisham' p.36-37 and 'Mother, any distance' p.52-53).

Chidiock Tichborne

Chidiock Tichborne (c.1558-1586) was a Roman Catholic. He was part of a plot to murder Elizabeth I and replace her with the Catholic Mary Queen of Scots. The plot was discovered and Chidiock was arrested and condemned to death. He wrote this poem in a letter to his wife, Agnes, just before his death. He was hung, drawn and quartered in 1586, at the age of 28.

Tichborne's Elegy

Written with his own hand in the Tower before his execution

> My prime of youth is but a frost of cares,
> My feast of joy is but a dish of pain;
> My crop of corn is but a field of tares,
> And all my good is but vain hope of gain.
> 5 The day is past, and yet I saw no sun;
> And now I live, and now my life is done.
>
> My tale was heard, and yet it was not told,
> My fruit is fallen, and yet my leaves are green;
> My youth is spent, and yet I am not old,
> 10 I saw the world, and yet I was not seen.
> My thread is cut, and yet it is not spun;
> And now I live, and now my life is done.
>
> I sought my death, and found it in my womb,
> I looked for life and saw it was a shade;
> 15 I trod the earth, and knew it was my tomb,
> And now I die, and now I was but made.
> My glass is full, and now my glass is run;
> And now I live, and now my life is done.

Annotations:
- This is supposed to be the best bit of his life.
- All these lines are phrased in the same way.
- He might be referring to his trial, or to the story of his life.
- The fallen fruit represents his death, the green leaves represent his youth.
- Nearly every word in the poem has just one syllable, making it sound plain and direct.
- He probably means an hourglass (he's running out of time).
- Gloomy language.
- The day represents life, the sun represents enjoyment of life.
- This line is repeated at the end of the other two verses as well.
- The repetition of "and yet" emphasises the irony of his situation — his life's over, and yet he's still young.
- The lines in this verse sound like riddles.
- Contrast: end of life and beginning of life.
- Very foreboding language — he's convinced he's going to die.
- The poem has a regular rhyme scheme.
- He hasn't got any hope.

POEM DICTIONARY
elegy — a song or verse commemorating a dead person
tares — weeds
shade — old-fashioned word for a ghost

Tichborne's Elegy

Chidiock Tichborne was about to be <u>executed</u> when he wrote this poem. Unsurprisingly, he's not too chuffed about the idea of <u>dying</u>. Little did he know that he would find everlasting life, in the pages of the GCSE AQA English Literature Anthology...

You've Got to Know What Happens in the Poem

<u>Lines 1-6</u>   Tichborne contrasts his <u>health and youth</u> with the fact that he's about to <u>die</u>.
He uses a series of metaphors to represent his situation.

<u>Lines 7-12</u>   Another verse on the <u>same theme</u>, also using metaphors.

<u>Lines 13-18</u> This verse is similar to the other two, but this one mentions <u>death</u> directly.
All three verses <u>end with the same line</u>, which sums up his predicament:
"And now I live, and now my life is done."

Learn About the Three Types of Language

1) <u>METAPHORICAL LANGUAGE</u> — Tichborne uses a series of <u>metaphors</u> throughout the poem to make the point that he's really young and healthy, and yet his life's over anyway.

2) <u>REPETITIVE LANGUAGE</u> — The poem is <u>structured</u> in a <u>repetitive</u> way, e.g. each verse ends with the same line. This emphasises his main point — that he's still young, but is about to die.

3) <u>LANGUAGE ABOUT DEATH</u> — Death is the main theme of the poem.
There's lots of <u>miserable language</u> and imagery about death.

Remember the Feelings and Attitudes in the Poem

1) <u>INJUSTICE</u> — He thinks it's <u>unfair</u> that he should have to die so young — he's being cut off in his prime.

2) <u>REGRET</u> — He feels <u>sad</u> that's he's got to leave life so soon.

3) <u>BITTERNESS</u> — There's a tiny bit of <u>bitterness</u> about his situation.

4) <u>IRONY</u> — It seems <u>ironic</u> to Tichborne that he's about to die even though he's young and he feels healthy.

Think About Your Feelings and Attitudes to the Poem

1) Pick 2 words or phrases that <u>stand out to you</u>. If none stand out, just pick 2 <u>unusual words or phrases</u>.

2) Write these 2 words or phrases down. Then write about how they <u>make you feel</u>. If they don't make you feel anything, don't worry — just <u>make something up</u>, as long as it's not too stupid.

> **EXAMPLE** I find the line "And now I live, and now my life is done" very moving. The poet's clear awareness of the hopelessness of his situation is tragic. Many people in that situation might be desperately hoping for escape and freedom, but Tichborne faces his fate. I think this is brave.

Themes — death, irony and mood...

You could compare 'Tichborne's Elegy' with other poems on the same theme: <u>death</u> ('November' p.58-59 and 'Hitcher' p.66-67), <u>irony</u> ('The Man He Killed' p.16-17 and 'Salome' p.42-43) and <u>mood</u> ('Sonnet' p.34-35 and 'I've made out a will' p.64-65).

Thomas Hardy

Thomas Hardy (1840-1928) was born in Dorset. He trained as an architect before becoming a very well-known novelist. He wrote classic and often controversial books like 'Jude the Obscure' and 'Far from the Madding Crowd', as well as writing poetry.

The Man He Killed

The whole poem's in speech marks — to make you imagine someone speaking out loud.

'Had he and I but met
By some old ancient inn,
We should have sat us down to wet
Right many a nipperkin!

The 1st and 3rd lines, and 2nd and 4th lines rhyme all the way through.

Informal, friendly language — contrasts with the description of the battle in the second verse.

5 'But ranged as infantry,
And staring face to face,
I shot at him as he at me,
And killed him in his place.

Very simple, straightforward description of dramatic event.

Repetition of 'because' shows he's stumbling to think of a reason why he killed the man.

'I shot him dead because –
10 Because he was my foe,
Just so: my foe of course he was;
That's clear enough; although

He tries to reassure himself that he was right to kill the man.

Shortened, colloquial version of "enlist" (to join the army).

'He thought he'd 'list, perhaps,
Off-hand like – just as I –

Informal language.

15 Was out of work – had sold his traps –
No other reason why.

The soldier imagines that the man he killed was similar to himself.

The man he killed probably wasn't evil or nasty — just an unemployed man who joined up because he needed a job.

'Yes; quaint and curious war is!
You shoot a fellow down

This line is worded almost like it's a joke — but there's a lot of bitterness in it.

Implies that everyone would do the same thing in a battle situation.

You'd treat if met where any bar is,
20 Or help to half-a-crown.'

Sounds more like a friend than an enemy.

POEM DICTIONARY
nipperkin — a small amount of beer or liquor
infantry — foot soldiers
foe — enemy
traps — belongings
help to — lend
half-a-crown — old British coin

The Man He Killed

In this poem, a <u>soldier</u> tells us about a man he <u>killed in battle</u>. He says that even though the man was on the opposing side, he was probably just a nice, ordinary bloke. He reckons that if he'd met the man in a pub, instead of the battlefield, they might have been <u>friends</u>.

You've Got to Know What Happens in the Poem

<u>Lines 1-4</u>	The soldier says that he could have been <u>friends</u> with the other man, if they had met in an <u>inn</u>.
<u>Lines 5-8</u>	But they met in <u>battle</u>, and shot at each other. The other man was <u>killed</u>.
<u>Lines 9-12</u>	The <u>only reason</u> he killed the other man was that they were <u>on different sides</u>.
<u>Lines 13-16</u>	He imagines that the man he killed may have been very <u>similar to him</u> — only enlisting in the army because he needed work.
<u>Lines 17-20</u>	He sums up the message of the poem. He says that <u>war is a strange business</u> — you kill people you might have been friends with in different circumstances.

Learn About the Three Types of Language

1) <u>COLLOQUIAL LANGUAGE</u> — This means <u>informal language</u> that sounds like everyday speech. The poem is written as if the soldier is speaking to the reader.

2) <u>MATTER-OF-FACT LANGUAGE</u> — The soldier uses fairly matter-of-fact, <u>down-to-earth</u> language to describe killing the man. This detached language <u>contrasts</u> with the serious message behind the poem, and helps to highlight the soldier's feeling of <u>bitterness</u>.

3) <u>THOUGHTFUL LANGUAGE</u> — The soldier thinks quite deeply about what he has done. He <u>empathises</u> with the man he killed.

Remember the Feelings and Attitudes in the Poem

Make beer, not war.

1) <u>IRONY</u> — The soldier has a <u>sense of irony</u> about the situation — he's killed a man who he might have been friends with in different circumstances.

2) <u>PUZZLEMENT</u> — It <u>troubles</u> the soldier that the man he killed was probably quite like himself.

3) <u>TRAGEDY</u> — The poet's <u>making a point</u> about the <u>tragedy of war</u>.

> Writing the poem from the point of view of an ordinary soldier increases the impact of the anti-war message.

Think About Your Feelings and Attitudes to the Poem

1) Pick 2 words or phrases that <u>stand out to you</u>. If none stand out, just pick 2 <u>unusual words or phrases</u>.

2) Write these 2 words or phrases down. Then write about how they <u>make you feel</u>. If they don't make you feel anything, don't worry — just <u>make something up</u>, as long as it's not too stupid.

> **EXAMPLE** The line "Yes; quaint and curious war is!" stands out to me because it's like an emotional outburst. All the way through the poem, the narrator sounds very restrained and matter-of-fact, and then suddenly there is this bitter, sarcastic statement. I can imagine the soldier spitting the words out.

Themes — death, irony and first person...

You can compare 'The Man He Killed' with other poems on the same themes: <u>death</u> ('Salome' p.42-43 and 'Education for Leisure' p.48-49), <u>irony</u> ('Tichborne's Elegy' p.14-15) and <u>use of first person</u> ('Ulysses' p.26-27 and 'Those bastards in their mansions' p.62-63).

Walt Whitman

Walt Whitman (1819-1892) was an American poet born in New York. He was one of America's earliest great poets, and was also a teacher and journalist.

Repeated to create a definite first impression of the storm.

An evil sound — dramatic and evil atmosphere.

The poem is one long sentence, with every line ending in "-ing" — this creates a sense of the storm happening right now, going on and on and on.

Patrolling Barnegat

Onomatopoeic description of the sea.

Alliteration of "s" suggests the sounds of the waves of the ocean.

Sharp and dangerous, like a sword.

The patrollers fear the worst.

A defensive force, protecting the land from the storm.

Makes the elements sound like an attacking force.

Sounds deep, rough and powerful.

Wild, wild the storm, and the sea high running,
Steady the roar of the gale, with incessant undertone muttering,
Shouts of demoniac laughter fitfully piercing and pealing,
Waves, air, midnight, their savagest trinity lashing,
5 Out in the shadows there milk-white combs careering,
On beachy slush and sand spirts of snow fierce slanting,
Where through the murk the easterly death-wind breasting,
Through cutting swirl and spray watchful and firm advancing,
(That in the distance! is that a wreck? is the red signal flaring?)
10 Slush and sand of the beach tireless till daylight wending,
Steadily, slowly, through hoarse roar never remitting,
Along the midnight edge by those milk-white combs careering,
A group of dim, weird forms, struggling, the night confronting,
That savage trinity warily watching.

The people in the patrol are hard to see in the confusion and chaos of the storm.

Like sentries on look-out.

Alliteration here sounds like the waves crashing down.

The patrollers face up to the enemy (the storm).

POEM DICTIONARY
Barnegat — a bay in New Jersey, USA
incessant — never-ending
demoniac — like the devil
pealing — making a long, loud sound
trinity — three things joined together
combs — the tops of waves
careering — moving quickly
breasting — facing, standing square-on
wending — travelling
remitting — stopping

Patrolling Barnegat

The poet describes a fierce <u>storm</u> blowing at night into a bay in America. Some people are <u>patrolling</u> the beach, standing up to the wild, cold wind. Brrrrrr....

You've Got to Know What Happens in the Poem

<u>Lines 1-6</u> A big <u>storm</u> is raging on a beach at night. Strong <u>winds</u> make massive <u>waves</u> in the sea which batter the land.

<u>Lines 7-14</u> Amid the dark and bleak night, people <u>patrol</u> the beach, facing up to the storm. They wonder if they can see a <u>shipwreck</u> in the distance (line 9).

Learn About the Two Types of Language

1) <u>WAR-LIKE LANGUAGE</u> — The storm is like a <u>battleground</u> between land and sea. The people on patrol on the beach are there to protect the land from attack.

2) <u>SOUNDS OF THE STORM</u> — There's lots of <u>alliteration</u> and <u>onomatopoeia</u> (words which sound like what they're describing). The poet uses these to create a sense of the <u>sounds</u> of the howling <u>wind</u> and roaring <u>waves</u>.

Remember the Feelings and Attitudes in the Poem

1) <u>RESPECT</u> — The poet <u>respects</u> the power of the storm.

2) <u>ADMIRATION</u> — He <u>admires</u> the bravery of the people patrolling the beach.

3) <u>WARINESS</u> — The people patrolling the beach are <u>cautious</u> (line 14).

> There's a sense of <u>dread</u> surrounding the storm — the storm seems capable of great destruction.

Think About Your Feelings and Attitudes to the Poem

1) Pick 2 words or phrases that <u>stand out to you</u>. If none stand out, just pick 2 <u>unusual words or phrases</u>.

2) Write these 2 words or phrases down. Then write about how they <u>make you feel</u>. If they don't make you feel anything, don't worry — just <u>make something up</u>, as long as it's not too stupid.

> **EXAMPLE** The description of the storm as a "savage trinity" fills me with fear. It sounds like a wild animal, with the three forces of the waves, air and night wildly attacking the land.

Themes — mood, danger and language effects...

Compare 'Patrolling Barnegat' with other poems on the same themes: <u>mood</u> ('We Remember Your Childhood Well' p.46-47), <u>danger</u> ('Stealing' p.50-51 and 'Those bastards in their mansions' p.62-63) and <u>language effects</u> ('The Eagle' p.24-25 and 'Inversnaid' p.32-33).

William Shakespeare

Key Poem

William Shakespeare (1564-1616) was a successful playwright and poet. He was born in Stratford-upon-Avon, Warwickshire, but lived in London for most of his life. He is one of the most important figures of Elizabethan literature.

Shakespeare wrote over 150 sonnets. This is the 130th.

These lines start as if they're going to be traditional compliments.

In most love poems, the woman would be compared favourably to these things.

This is the big turning point in the poem. He does love something about her.

He's says he's never seen a goddess, so can't compare her to one. This is a bit of a dig at traditional love poetry, where women are praised unrealistically.

The last two lines are inset, making them stand out.

Sonnet 130

My mistress' eyes are nothing like the sun;
Coral is far more red than her lips' red.
If snow be white, why then her breasts are dun;
If hairs be wires, black wires grow on her head.
5 I have seen roses damasked, red and white,
But no such roses see I in her cheeks;
And in some perfumes is there more delight
Than in the breath that from my mistress reeks.
I love to hear her speak, yet well I know
10 That music hath a far more pleasing sound.
I grant I never saw a goddess go:
My mistress when she walks treads on the ground.
    And yet, by heaven, I think my love as rare
    As any she belied with false compare.

The word "nothing" changes this line from a compliment into a criticism.

These words might be found in a normal love poem.

Sounds ugly and coarse. The opposite of saying someone has hair like gold.

Alternate lines rhyme for the first 12 lines.

This woman's real — not some romantic ideal.

The sonnet ends with a rhyming couplet.

Any woman.

This exclamation shows real feeling. He does love her after all.

POEM DICTIONARY
dun — a brownish-grey colour
damasked — damask roses are a type of sweet-smelling rose, damask is a type of embroidered fabric
reeks — breathes out, smells
belied — misrepresented, shown to be false

Sonnet 130

Shakespeare spends most of the poem <u>criticising</u> his lover — she's not beautiful, she smells, her hair's all coarse like wire... Then he turns it all around by saying he <u>loves her</u> anyway. You have to hope she was the forgiving sort.

You've Got to Know What Happens in the Poem

<u>Lines 1-4</u>	He makes blunt, <u>critical statements</u> about his mistress's looks. She doesn't match up to popular ideas of beauty in Elizabethan times, e.g. she's dark-haired, not fair.
<u>Lines 5-12</u>	He lists more beautiful things (roses, music, perfume, goddesses) but then explains that she <u>isn't</u> like any of these either. On line 9, however, it starts to become apparent that <u>he does like her really</u>.
<u>Lines 13-14</u>	In the <u>final rhyming couplet</u>, he says that he thinks his mistress is <u>great</u> — as good as any other woman who's been praised in love poetry.

Learn About the Three Types of Language

1) <u>SUBVERSION OF TRADITIONAL IMAGES OF BEAUTY</u> — Many of the lines sound like they're going to be traditional images of women's beauty. But Shakespeare goes <u>against the reader's expectations</u> by saying that his mistress isn't like these images — she's beautiful in a more <u>genuine</u> way.

2) <u>CRITICAL LANGUAGE</u> — He sounds <u>pretty scathing</u> about his mistress in the first part of the poem.

3) <u>SONNET FORM</u> — The poem is in traditional sonnet form. It has <u>fourteen lines</u> and is in <u>iambic pentameters</u> (see glossary). Sonnets are often used for <u>love poetry</u>.

Remember the Feelings and Attitudes in the Poem

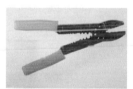

Time for a hair cut.

1) <u>SUBVERSION</u> — Shakespeare's <u>having fun</u> with this poem, turning the reader's expectations of a love poem on their head.

2) <u>CONTEMPT</u> — He sounds pretty <u>insulting</u> about his mistress's looks, voice and smell in the first part of the poem.

3) <u>LOVE</u> — Then at the end, the message seems to be: "I <u>love her</u> warts and all. I don't need to pretend she's a goddess."

> Shakespeare wrote a lot of traditional love sonnets, where he would compare women to roses etc. So in a way he's <u>taking the mick out of his own poetry</u> in Sonnet 130.

Think About Your Feelings and Attitudes to the Poem

1) Pick 2 words or phrases that <u>stand out to you</u>. If none stand out, just pick 2 <u>unusual words or phrases</u>.

2) Write these 2 words or phrases down. Then write about how they <u>make you feel</u>. If they don't make you feel anything, don't worry — just <u>make something up</u>, as long as it's not too stupid.

> **EXAMPLE** I really like the phrase "belied with false compare." Often when I read love poetry it does seem pretty false: no one really floats like a goddess or has a voice sweeter than music. The conclusion to this poem is surprisingly down-to-earth and realistic.

Themes — love, imagery and closing couplets...

You can compare this poem other poems on the same themes: <u>love</u> ('Anne Hathaway' p.40-41), <u>imagery</u> ('Patrolling Barnegat' p.18-19 and 'I've made out a will' p.64-65) and <u>closing couplets</u> ('The Village Schoolmaster' p.28-29 and 'Havisham' p.36-37).

Robert Browning

The Duke's jealous — he suggests the Duchess flirted with everyone.

He's proud of his history, his important family and the titles of "Duke" and "Duchess".

30 She rode with round the terrace – all and each
Would draw from her alike the approving speech,
Or blush, at least. She thanked men, – good! but thanked–
Somehow – I know not how – as if she ranked
My gift of a nine-hundred-years-old name
With anybody's gift. Who'd stoop to blame
35 This sort of trifling? Even had you skill
In speech – (which I have not) – to make your will
Quite clear to such a one, and say, 'Just this
'Or that in you disgusts me; here you miss,
'Or there exceed the mark' – and if she let
40 Herself be lessoned so, nor plainly set
Her wits to yours, forsooth and made excuse,
– E'en then would be some stooping; and I choose
Never to stoop. Oh sir, she smiled, no doubt,
Whene'er I passed her; but who passed without
45 Much the same smile? This grew; I gave commands;
Then all smiles stopped together. There she stands
As if alive. Will't please you to rise? We'll meet
The company below, then. I repeat,
The Count your master's known munificence
50 Is ample warrant that no just pretence
Of mine for dowry will be disallowed;
Though his fair daughter's self, as I avowed
At starting, is my object. Nay, we'll go
Together down, sir. Notice Neptune, though,
55 Taming a sea-horse, thought a rarity,
Which Claus of Innsbruck cast in bronze for me.

He says you shouldn't judge people — but it seems he couldn't help it.

He thinks spoken criticism is beneath him — suggests he found some other way of dealing with the problem.

He doesn't explain how this happened, which makes it sound sinister.

The Duke reminds his visitor of his low status.

Moves onto another valuable possession as if he's said nothing unusual.

False modesty — he clearly does like speaking.

This word suggests he was more bothered about the Duchess's behaviour than he's letting on.

He sounds suspicious of her — maybe he thought she was being unfaithful.

Shows his power — but we don't find out what the commands were.

He's arranging his next marriage — his Next Duchess.

Sounds polite, but he's definitely in charge.

POEM DICTIONARY
countenance — face
durst — dare
mantle — cloak
bough — branch
forsooth — indeed
officious — fawning
munificence — generosity
dowry — money paid to a man by his bride's family when they marry
avowed — said
Neptune — Roman god of the sea

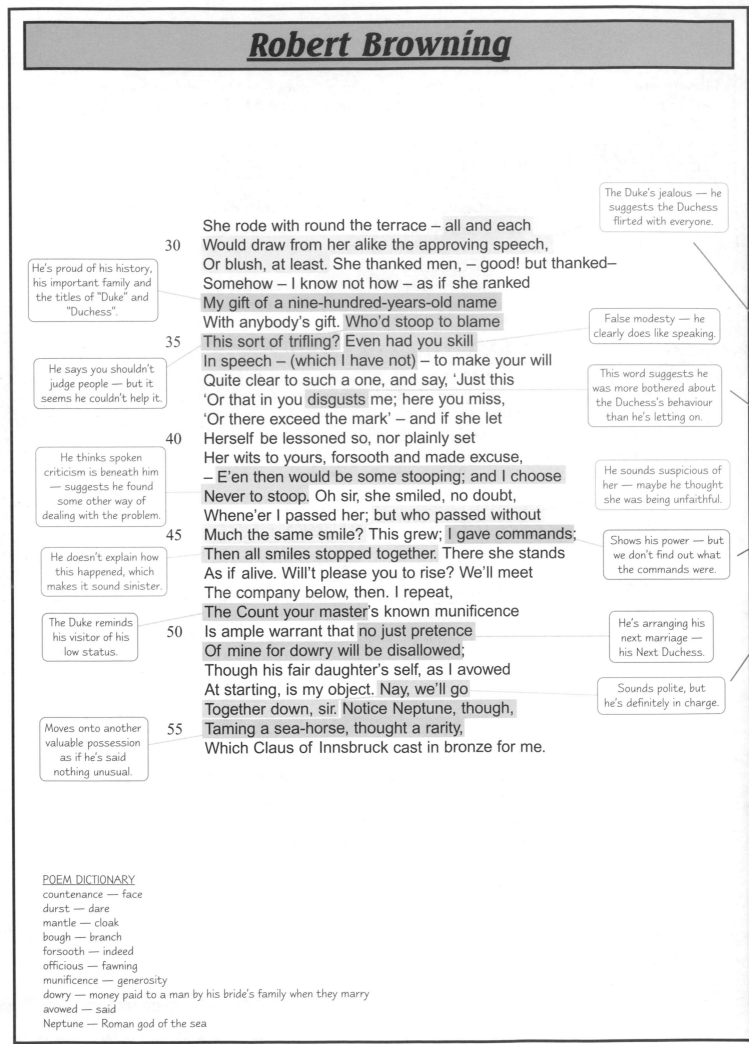

Robert Browning

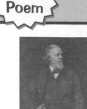

Robert Browning (1812-1889) was born in Camberwell, Surrey. He read and wrote poems from an early age. He married Elizabeth Barrett, another well-known poet. He produced many collections of poems, before he died in Venice, Italy.

My Last Duchess

Ferrara

The name of a 16th century Duke.

Sets a sinister tone.

Sounds polite, but he's really being quite forceful here.

He controls who looks at the painting — but he couldn't control who looked at his wife when she was alive.

Reference to death is out of place and suspicious.

The Duke struggles to express his irritation.

She was cheery and friendly — but the Duke means this as a criticism.

He sounds like he's justifying himself — he's on the defensive.

That's my last Duchess painted on the wall,
Looking as if she were alive. I call
That piece a wonder, now: Frà Pandolf's hands
Worked busily a day, and there she stands.
5   Will't please you sit and look at her? I said
'Frà Pandolf' by design, for never read
Strangers like you that pictured countenance,
The depth and passion of its earnest glance,
But to myself they turned (since none puts by
10 The curtain I have drawn for you, but I)
And seemed as they would ask me, if they durst
How such a glance came there; so, not the first
Are you to turn and ask thus. Sir, 'twas not
Her husband's presence only, called that spot
15 Of joy into the Duchess' cheek: perhaps
Frà Pandolf chanced to say 'Her mantle laps
'Over my lady's wrist too much,' or 'Paint
'Must never hope to reproduce the faint
'Half-flush that dies along her throat:' such stuff
20 Was courtesy, she thought, and cause enough
For calling up that spot of joy. She had
A heart — how shall I say? — too soon made glad,
Too easily impressed; she liked whate'er
She looked on, and her looks went everywhere.
25 Sir, 'twas all one! My favour at her breast,
The dropping of the daylight in the West,
The bough of cherries some officious fool
Broke in the orchard for her, the white mule

Sounds like he owns the Duchess herself, not just the picture of her.

The name of the artist.

The portrait shows she had strong emotions.

Suggests people were scared of his temper.

Creates the impression of a question from the visitor.

Repeating this shows it bothers him.

She flirted a lot — the Duke thinks so anyway.

THIS IS A FLAP.
FOLD THIS PAGE OUT.

My Last Duchess

In this poem, a Duke is talking to a visitor about a <u>portrait</u> of his wife, who is now dead. He says he really likes the picture, but then he goes on about how she used to <u>smile</u> and have a laugh with everyone, and this annoyed him. We begin to suspect her death may have been a bit <u>suspicious</u>.

You've Got to Know What Happens in the Poem

<u>Lines 1-5</u> The Duke points out the <u>portrait</u> of the Duchess to a visitor. He's very <u>proud</u> of it.

<u>Lines 5-13</u> He says people always ask him about the <u>passionate expression</u> on the Duchess's face.

<u>Lines 13-21</u> The Duke says the Duchess's flirty expression <u>wasn't</u> reserved <u>just for him</u>.

<u>Lines 21-34</u> He says she <u>smiled at everyone</u>. He's annoyed that she treated him just like <u>anyone else</u>.

<u>Lines 34-43</u> He says it would have been <u>wrong</u> to <u>criticise</u> her for her behaviour.

<u>Lines 43-47</u> He acted to <u>stop</u> the Duchess's <u>flirting</u> — but, suspiciously, he doesn't say <u>how</u> he did this.

<u>Lines 47-56</u> The Duke and his guest <u>walk away</u> from the painting. The Duke reveals he's planning to get <u>married again</u>, this time to the daughter of a Count.

Learn About the Four Types of Language

1) <u>JEALOUS LANGUAGE</u> — The things the Duke says about the Duchess sound quite innocent at first. But we can read <u>hidden meanings</u> into them which hint at the Duke's <u>jealousy</u>, e.g. by saying she <u>smiled</u> a lot, he seems to suggest that she was a <u>flirt</u>, and maybe <u>unfaithful</u> to him.

2) <u>SINISTER LANGUAGE</u> — The Duke sometimes says things that make him sound a bit <u>sinister</u> — there's a <u>dark side</u> to him. We begin to suspect that he might have <u>killed</u> the Duchess.

3) <u>LANGUAGE ABOUT POWER</u> — The Duke feels the need to have <u>power</u> and <u>control</u> over the Duchess. He sees her as another of his <u>possessions</u>, just like his expensive paintings.

4) <u>FORMAL LANGUAGE</u> — The Duke talks in a <u>polite</u>, old-fashioned way. He sometimes uses this to <u>cover up</u> the fact that he says some pretty <u>nasty</u> and <u>suspicious</u> things.

Remember the Feelings and Attitudes in the Poem

"The brazen hussy..."

1) <u>PRIDE</u> — The Duke is very proud of his <u>possessions</u> and his <u>status</u>.

2) <u>JEALOUSY</u> — He <u>couldn't stand</u> the way the Duchess treated him <u>no better</u> than anyone else (lines 31-34).

3) <u>POWER</u> — The Duke enjoys the <u>control</u> he has over the painting (lines 9-10). He didn't have this power over the Duchess when she was alive.

Think About Your Feelings and Attitudes to the Poem

1) Pick 2 words or phrases that <u>stand out to you</u>. If none stand out, just pick 2 <u>unusual words or phrases</u>.

2) Write these 2 words or phrases down. Then write about how they <u>make you feel</u>. If they don't make you feel anything, don't worry — just <u>make something up</u>, as long as it's not too stupid.

> **EXAMPLE** When the Duke says "all smiles stopped together", I'm very suspicious of the Duke. His tone suggests he was satisfied with the result of his "commands". Considering the Duchess is now dead, this seems rather sinister to me.

Themes — attitudes towards others, evil and first person...

You should compare this poem with other poems about the same themes: <u>attitudes towards other people</u> ('Havisham' p.36-37), <u>evil</u> ('The Laboratory' p.30-31 and 'Education for Leisure' p.48-49) and <u>use of first person</u> ('Elvis's Twin Sister' p.38-39 and 'Hitcher' p.66-67).

Alfred Tennyson

Alfred Tennyson (1809-1892) was born in Lincolnshire and later lived on the Isle of Wight and in Surrey. He studied at Trinity College, Cambridge. Tennyson was one of the great poets of the Victorian era and was Poet Laureate from 1850 to 1892.

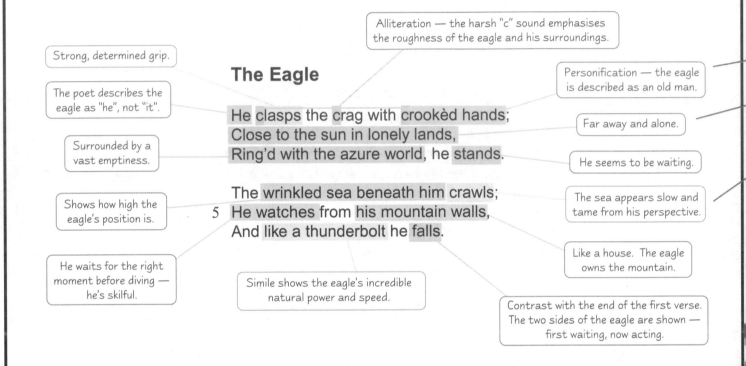

Alliteration — the harsh "c" sound emphasises the roughness of the eagle and his surroundings.

Strong, determined grip.

Personification — the eagle is described as an old man.

The poet describes the eagle as "he", not "it".

Far away and alone.

Surrounded by a vast emptiness.

He seems to be waiting.

Shows how high the eagle's position is.

The sea appears slow and tame from his perspective.

He waits for the right moment before diving — he's skilful.

Like a house. The eagle owns the mountain.

Simile shows the eagle's incredible natural power and speed.

Contrast with the end of the first verse. The two sides of the eagle are shown — first waiting, now acting.

The Eagle

He clasps the crag with crookèd hands;
Close to the sun in lonely lands,
Ring'd with the azure world, he stands.

The wrinkled sea beneath him crawls;
5 He watches from his mountain walls,
And like a thunderbolt he falls.

POEM DICTIONARY
azure — blue

The Eagle

The poet describes a magnificent <u>eagle</u>. That's it.

You've Got to Know What Happens in the Poem

<u>Lines 1-3</u>   The eagle stands on a <u>cliff</u>, in front of the sun and surrounded by the big blue <u>sky</u>.

<u>Lines 4-6</u>   The eagle patiently watches the <u>sea</u>, then <u>dives</u> into it for food, quick as a flash.

Learn About the Three Types of Language

1) <u>PERSONIFICATION</u> — The poet describes the eagle as if it's a <u>person</u> he respects — e.g. he says "him" rather that "it". The eagle is like an admirable <u>old man</u>.

2) <u>ISOLATION</u> — The eagle is <u>alone</u> and <u>unique</u>. He belongs to the <u>sky</u> around him, not the earth way below.

3) <u>POWERFUL LANGUAGE</u> — The eagle is <u>strong</u> and <u>fast</u>. He's the king of everything he sees.

> The rhyming triplets and regular rhythm create an impression of the natural beauty of the scene.

Remember the Feelings and Attitudes in the Poem

"Here, fishy-fishy..."

1) <u>RESPECT</u> — The poet <u>respects</u> the magnificent <u>strong figure</u> of the eagle, perched on the cliff.

2) <u>ADMIRATION</u> — He also <u>admires</u> the physical <u>speed</u> and <u>power</u> of the eagle when he dives towards the sea.

> Lines 1-3 show how great the eagle looks just <u>standing there</u>. Lines 4-6 show how good he looks <u>in action</u>.

Think About Your Feelings and Attitudes to the Poem

1) Pick 2 words or phrases that <u>stand out to you</u>. If none stand out, just pick 2 <u>unusual words or phrases</u>.

2) Write these 2 words or phrases down. Then write about how they <u>make you feel</u>. If they don't make you feel anything, don't worry — just <u>make something up</u>, as long as it's not too stupid.

> **EXAMPLE** The simile "like a thunderbolt" makes me feel amazed at the eagle's speed. His dive happens in a flash, almost too quick to see, but also with great power.

Themes — language effects and imagery...

Compare 'The Eagle' with other poems about the same themes: <u>language effects</u> ('Inversnaid' p.32-33, 'Sonnet' p.34-35 and 'Stealing' p.50-51) and <u>imagery</u> 'The Little Boy Lost'/'The Little Boy Found' p.12-13, 'Elvis's Twin Sister' p.38-39 and 'Homecoming' p.56-57).

Alfred Tennyson

The seas are dark and intimidating — this seems to add to their appeal.

He reminds his crew of their past achievements.

45   There lies in the port; the vessel puffs her sail:
     There gloom the dark broad seas. My mariners,
     Souls that have toiled, and wrought, and thought with me —
     That ever was a frolic welcome took
     The thunder and the sunshine, and opposed
     Free hearts, free foreheads — you and I are old;
50   Old age hath yet his honour and his toil;
     Death closes all: but something ere the end,
     Some work of noble note, may yet be done,
     Not unbecoming men that strove with Gods.
     The lights begin to twinkle from the rocks:
55   The long day wanes: the slow moon climbs: the deep
     Moans round with many voices. Come, my friends,
     'Tis not too late to seek a newer world.
     Push off, and sitting well in order smite
     The sounding furrows; for my purpose holds
60   To sail beyond the sunset, and the baths
     Of all the western stars, until I die.
     It may be that the gulfs will wash us down:
     It may be we shall touch the Happy Isles,
     And see the great Achilles, whom we knew.
65   Though much is taken, much abides; and though
     We are not now that strength which in old days
     Moved earth and heaven; that which we are, we are;
     One equal temper of heroic hearts,
     Made weak by time and fate, but strong in will
70   To strive, to seek, to find and not to yield.

He reminds his mariners that they don't have much time left in life.

He's realistic — just because he's a hero, he doesn't think he's invincible.

The end of the day symbolises the end of their lifetimes.

He feels the sea is calling him away.

Talks to the seamen as his equals.

These phrases suggest he's talking about the afterlife.

Another reminder that death isn't far away.

He tells his band of men that he's united with them, to make them feel ready to set off together.

Ulysses ends his speech with a rousing flourish, to stir his crew.

POEM DICTIONARY
Ulysses — Roman name for Odysseus, a Greek hero who fought in the Trojan War and spent 10 years travelling home
mete and dole — give out
lees — last drops
Hyades — in Greek mythology, the seven daughters of Atlas
vext — angered
unburnished — unpolished
Telemachus — son of Ulysses
sceptre — symbol of ruling power
prudence — care, caution
mariners — sailors
ere — before
strove — fought
smite — strike
furrows — trenches
Achilles — another Greek hero
abides — remains

THIS IS A FLAP.
FOLD THIS PAGE OUT

Alfred Tennyson

Ulysses

The plodding rhythm in this verse reflects his boredom and frustration.

Drab, down-to-earth setting.

It little profits that an idle king,
By this still hearth, among these barren crags,
Matched with an agèd wife, I mete and dole
Unequal laws unto a savage race,
5   That hoard, and sleep, and feed, and know not me.

This sums up his attitude.

He's determined to use up every last second of life.

I cannot rest from travel: I will drink
Life to the lees: all times I have enjoyed
Greatly, have suffered greatly, both with those
That loved me, and alone; on shore, and when
10   Through scudding drifts the rainy Hyades

He knows he's famous.

Vext the dim sea; I am become a name;

He's proud and confident.

For always roaming with a hungry heart

Alliteration adds to the sense of eagerness.

Much have I seen and known; cities of men
And manners, climates, councils, governments,

Describes how warriors become intoxicated with the excitement of battle.

15   Myself not least, but honoured of them all;

The ancient city where the Trojan War was fought.

And drunk delight of battle with my peers,
Far on the ringing plains of windy Troy.
I am a part of all that I have met;

Suggests he belongs in other places, not just his original home.

Each adventure makes you realise how many more adventures there are out there — you never feel like you've done everything.

Yet all experience is an arch wherethrough
20   Gleams that untravelled world, whose margin fades
For ever and for ever when I move.
How dull it is to pause, to make an end,

He feels useless and bored when he's resting.

To rust unburnished, not to shine in use!

Compares himself to a sword, rusting through lack of use.

As though to breathe were life. Life piled on life
25   Were all too little, and of one to me

He does not have enough time left to do all the things he wants to do.

Little remains: but every hour is saved
From that eternal silence, something more,
A bringer of new things; and vile it were
For some three suns to store and hoard myself,
30   And to this gray spirit yearning in desire

He's desperate for new experiences.

To follow knowledge like a sinking star,

He wants to carry on travelling forever — his journey will never be complete.

Beyond the utmost bound of human thought.

This is my son, mine own Telemachus,
To whom I leave the sceptre and the isle –
35   Well-loved of me, discerning to fulfil
This labour, by slow prudence to make mild

Descriptions of his son's duties contrast with the excitement of Ulysses' adventures.

A rugged people, and through soft degrees
Subdue them to the useful and the good.
Most blameless is he, centred in the sphere
40   Of common duties, decent not to fail
In offices of tenderness, and pay
Meet adoration to my household gods,

He's going on a voyage but also facing up to death.

When I am gone. He works his work, I mine.

He and his son are different kinds of people.

Ulysses

This poem is about the ancient Greek hero <u>Ulysses</u>. He's returned from the Trojan War to rule his home island of Ithaca as King — but he feels restless. He decides he needs to spend the rest of his life having <u>more adventures</u>. The poem ends with a rousing speech to his crew.

You've Got to Know What Happens in the Poem

<u>Lines 1-5</u>   Ulysses has returned home. He feels <u>frustrated</u> and <u>bored</u> ruling his "savage" people.

<u>Lines 6-32</u>   He decides he has to <u>continue his adventures</u> right up to his dying day. He remembers his past adventures and says there's <u>no point</u> in just sitting about — he has to get all he can out of life.

<u>Lines 33-43</u> He talks about his <u>son</u>, Telemachus. He says Telemachus is less adventurous, but he'll make a <u>good ruler</u>. Ulysses is proud of him — but he's a <u>different</u> kind of person from Ulysses.

<u>Lines 44-61</u> Ulysses addresses his <u>crew</u> before they set off on their voyage. He says that he and they may be <u>old</u>, but they're brave and strong men who are still capable of new <u>achievements</u>.

<u>Lines 62-70</u> Ulysses <u>motivates his crew</u>. He tells them that they're not as strong as they once were, and they may not come back alive, but they're <u>brave men</u> who will give their all.

Learn About the Four Types of Language

1) <u>HEROIC LANGUAGE</u> — Ulysses proudly describes his exciting <u>adventures</u>. He uses stirring, heroic language to <u>fire up</u> his crew before their next voyage.

2) <u>IMAGERY</u> — Ulysses creates some <u>powerful images</u> of his battles and adventures.

3) <u>LANGUAGE ABOUT DEATH</u> — He's well aware that he's <u>old</u>, and this makes him determined to <u>get the most</u> out of the time he has left. He mentions <u>death</u> several times, but he doesn't seem scared of dying.

4) <u>LANGUAGE ABOUT FRUSTRATION</u> — He feels bored and frustrated when he's not active.

Remember the Feelings and Attitudes in the Poem

1) <u>BOREDOM</u> — Ulysses feels <u>bored</u> by the thought of ruling his people at home. He seems <u>scornful</u> of them: "a savage race".

2) <u>PRIDE</u> — Ulysses is <u>proud</u> of his brave reputation and his great achievements in the past.

3) <u>EXCITEMENT</u> — He <u>looks forward</u> to the coming voyage and uses his own excitement to <u>inspire</u> his crew.

Think About Your Feelings and Attitudes to the Poem

1) Pick 2 words or phrases that <u>stand out to you</u>. If none stand out, just pick 2 <u>unusual words or phrases</u>.

2) Write these 2 words or phrases down. Then write about how they <u>make you feel</u>. If they don't make you feel anything, don't worry — just <u>make something up</u>, as long as it's not too stupid.

> **EXAMPLE**   I really respect Ulysses' courage when he says "my purpose holds / To sail beyond the sunset". This line shows he is determined to continue his adventures for as long as possible, and he is not afraid of death.

Themes — death, memory and getting older...

You could compare 'Ulysses' with other poems about the same themes: <u>death</u> ('Tichborne's Elegy p.14-15, 'The Man He Killed' p.16-17 and 'November' p.58-59), <u>memory</u> ('The Village Schoolmaster p.28-29) and <u>getting older</u> ('November' p.58-59 and 'Kid' p.60-61).

Oliver Goldsmith

<u>Oliver Goldsmith</u> (1728-1774) was an Irish playwright and poet. He studied at Trinity College, Dublin. He was also a translator and wrote children's books and histories.

The Village Schoolmaster

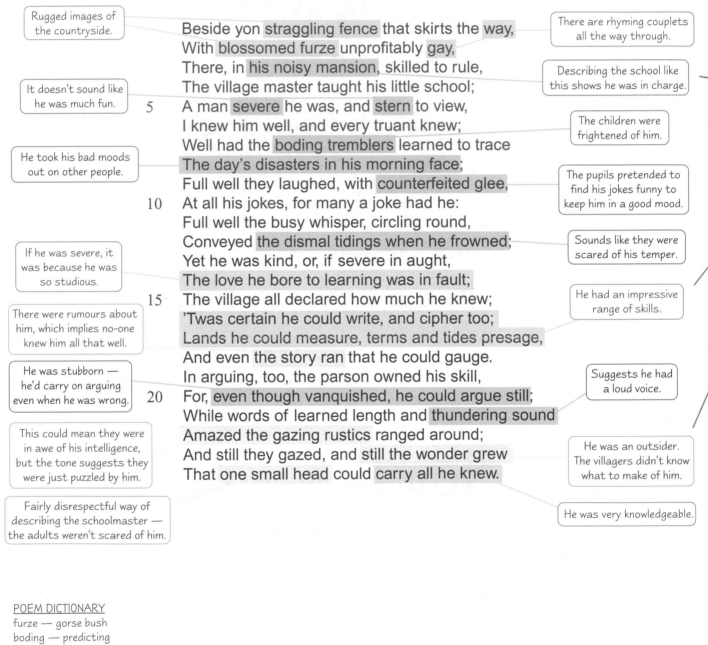

Rugged images of the countryside.

There are rhyming couplets all the way through.

It doesn't sound like he was much fun.

Describing the school like this shows he was in charge.

The children were frightened of him.

He took his bad moods out on other people.

The pupils pretended to find his jokes funny to keep him in a good mood.

If he was severe, it was because he was so studious.

Sounds like they were scared of his temper.

There were rumours about him, which implies no-one knew him all that well.

He had an impressive range of skills.

He was stubborn — he'd carry on arguing even when he was wrong.

Suggests he had a loud voice.

This could mean they were in awe of his intelligence, but the tone suggests they were just puzzled by him.

He was an outsider. The villagers didn't know what to make of him.

Fairly disrespectful way of describing the schoolmaster — the adults weren't scared of him.

He was very knowledgeable.

Beside yon straggling fence that skirts the way,
With blossomed furze unprofitably gay,
There, in his noisy mansion, skilled to rule,
The village master taught his little school;
5 A man severe he was, and stern to view,
I knew him well, and every truant knew;
Well had the boding tremblers learned to trace
The day's disasters in his morning face;
Full well they laughed, with counterfeited glee,
10 At all his jokes, for many a joke had he:
Full well the busy whisper, circling round,
Conveyed the dismal tidings when he frowned;
Yet he was kind, or, if severe in aught,
The love he bore to learning was in fault;
15 The village all declared how much he knew;
'Twas certain he could write, and cipher too;
Lands he could measure, terms and tides presage,
And even the story ran that he could gauge.
In arguing, too, the parson owned his skill,
20 For, even though vanquished, he could argue still;
While words of learned length and thundering sound
Amazed the gazing rustics ranged around;
And still they gazed, and still the wonder grew
That one small head could carry all he knew.

<u>POEM DICTIONARY</u>
furze — gorse bush
boding — predicting
counterfeited — faked
aught — anything
cipher — count, do arithmetic
presage — forecast
gauge — measure
rustics — people who live in the countryside

The Village Schoolmaster

This poem is about the old <u>schoolmaster</u> of a village school. He was a rather strange bloke — he was bad-tempered and a bit <u>frightening</u>, but also very <u>intelligent</u> and skilful. Although the poet doesn't say it outright, it seems that the people in the village thought he was a bit of an oddball.

You've Got to Know What Happens in the Poem

Lines 1-12   The poet points out a place in the <u>countryside</u> where a village school was. Then we hear about how <u>strict</u> the schoolmaster was — he was often in a <u>bad mood</u> and the pupils were <u>scared</u> of him.

Lines 13-24   Then the poet says how <u>clever</u> the schoolmaster was. He had loads of different <u>skills</u>. The villagers were <u>amazed</u> by how much he knew — although they didn't seem to like him very much.

Learn About the Three Types of Language

1) <u>INTIMIDATING LANGUAGE</u> — The way the schoolmaster looked and acted makes him seem <u>scary</u> and <u>unpleasant</u>. The children were afraid of his <u>temper</u>, and laughed at his rubbish jokes to avoid getting on the wrong side of him.

2) <u>LANGUAGE ABOUT EDUCATION</u> — The schoolmaster had all sorts of <u>skills</u> and <u>knowledge</u>. The villagers were <u>amazed</u> at how much he knew.

3) <u>MYSTERY</u> — He was an <u>outsider</u> and a <u>loner</u>. The people in the village didn't know much about him and seemed to think he was a bit <u>odd</u>, rather than respecting him.

Remember the Feelings and Attitudes in the Poem

"Today, children, you're going to learn about how great I am."

1) <u>FEAR</u> — The children were <u>scared</u> of the schoolmaster.

2) <u>FASCINATION</u> — The villagers were <u>fascinated</u> by the schoolmaster, but they <u>didn't respect</u> him very much (lines 23-24).

3) <u>MOCKERY</u> — The poet seems to <u>mock</u> the school master — he creates an impression of him being a <u>pompous show-off</u> (although he doesn't openly say this).

Think About Your Feelings and Attitudes to the Poem

1) Pick 2 words or phrases that <u>stand out to you</u>. If none stand out, just pick 2 <u>unusual words or phrases</u>.

2) Write these 2 words or phrases down. Then write about how they <u>make you feel</u>. If they don't make you feel anything, don't worry — just <u>make something up</u>, as long as it's not too stupid.

> **EXAMPLE** The description of the schoolmaster as having "The day's disasters in his morning face" makes him sound scary and intimidating. I wouldn't want to have him as my headteacher.

Themes — characters, closing couplets, memory...

Compare 'The Village Schoolmaster' with other poems on the same themes: <u>characters</u> (Ulysses p.26-27 and 'Kid' p.60-61), <u>closing couplets</u> ('Havisham' p.36-37 and 'I've made out a will' p.64-65) and <u>memory</u> ('We Remember Your Childhood Well' p.46-47 and 'Homecoming' p.56-57).

Robert Browning

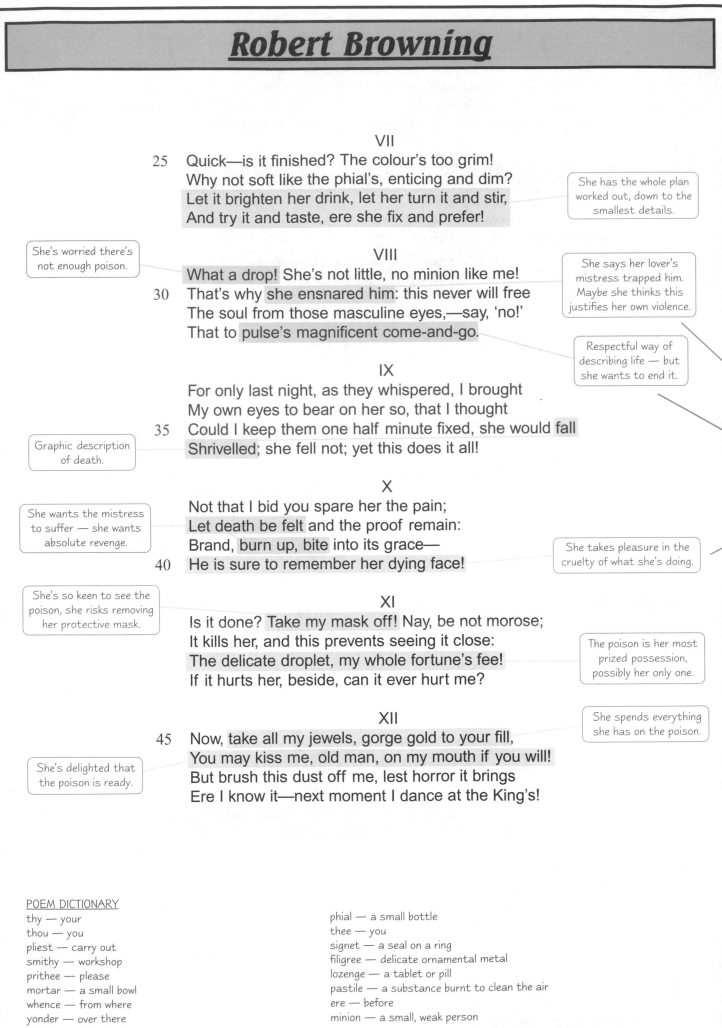

VII

25   Quick—is it finished? The colour's too grim!
Why not soft like the phial's, enticing and dim?
Let it brighten her drink, let her turn it and stir,
And try it and taste, ere she fix and prefer!

She has the whole plan worked out, down to the smallest details.

VIII

She's worried there's not enough poison.

What a drop! She's not little, no minion like me!
30   That's why she ensnared him: this never will free
The soul from those masculine eyes,—say, 'no!'
That to pulse's magnificent come-and-go.

She says her lover's mistress trapped him. Maybe she thinks this justifies her own violence.

Respectful way of describing life — but she wants to end it.

IX

For only last night, as they whispered, I brought
My own eyes to bear on her so, that I thought
35   Could I keep them one half minute fixed, she would fall
Shrivelled; she fell not; yet this does it all!

Graphic description of death.

X

She wants the mistress to suffer — she wants absolute revenge.

Not that I bid you spare her the pain;
Let death be felt and the proof remain:
Brand, burn up, bite into its grace—
40   He is sure to remember her dying face!

She takes pleasure in the cruelty of what she's doing.

XI

She's so keen to see the poison, she risks removing her protective mask.

Is it done? Take my mask off! Nay, be not morose;
It kills her, and this prevents seeing it close:
The delicate droplet, my whole fortune's fee!
If it hurts her, beside, can it ever hurt me?

The poison is her most prized possession, possibly her only one.

XII

She spends everything she has on the poison.

45   Now, take all my jewels, gorge gold to your fill,
You may kiss me, old man, on my mouth if you will!
But brush this dust off me, lest horror it brings
Ere I know it—next moment I dance at the King's!

She's delighted that the poison is ready.

POEM DICTIONARY

thy — your	phial — a small bottle
thou — you	thee — you
pliest — carry out	signet — a seal on a ring
smithy — workshop	filigree — delicate ornamental metal
prithee — please	lozenge — a tablet or pill
mortar — a small bowl	pastile — a substance burnt to clean the air
whence — from where	ere — before
yonder — over there	minion — a small, weak person

The Laboratory

ANCIEN RÉGIME

This tells us that the poem is set in France, in the days when they had a monarchy.

I

Now that I, tying thy glass mask tightly,
May gaze thro' these faint smokes curling whitely,
As thou pliest thy trade in this devil's-smithy—
Which is the poison to poison her, prithee?

She wears a mask for safety.

She knows what she's doing is evil.

II

5   He is with her, and they know that I know
Where they are, what they do: they believe my tears flow
While they laugh, laugh at me, at me fled to the drear
Empty church, to pray God in, for them! —I am here.

She's paranoid that she's a laughing stock — this makes her more determined to get revenge.

The whole poem is in rhyming couplets.

III

Grind away, moisten and mash up thy paste,
10   Pound at thy powder,—I am not in haste!
Better sit thus, and observe thy strange things,
Than go where men wait me and dance at the King's.

The way she describes making the poison shows her violent feelings — she'd like to do these things to her rival.

Their lives are based around the Royal Court.

IV

That in the mortar—you call it a gum?
Ah, the brave tree whence such gold oozings come!
15   And yonder soft phial, the exquisite blue,
Sure to taste sweetly,—is that poison too?

She wants to know how the poison is made, and where the ingredients come from.

The poison is precious to her.

The colour of the poison is beautiful to her.

V

Had I but all of them, thee and thy treasures,
What a wild crowd of invisible pleasures!
To carry pure death in an earring, a casket,
20   A signet, a fan-mount, a filigree basket!

There's no doubt about what she wants to happen.

The potions are rare and valuable.

She gets carried away with excitement, listing all the things she can think of that could hold poison.

VI

Soon, at the King's, a mere lozenge to give,
And Pauline should have just thirty minutes to live!
But to light a pastile, and Elise, with her head
And her breast and her arms and her hands, should drop dead!

There's a dark humour here — usually people would use these to make things better.

The idea of killing excites her.

THIS IS A FLAP.
FOLD THIS PAGE OUT. →

The Laboratory

This poem's set in France, back in the days when posh people lived at the <u>King's Court</u>.
The woman's at a drug shop to get some <u>poison</u> so she can kill her lover's mistress
and some other women who she reckons are after her lover. Seems a trifle extreme...

You've Got to Know What Happens in the Poem

<u>Lines 1-4</u>	The woman talks to the chemist while he <u>mixes the poison</u> in his workshop.
<u>Lines 5-8</u>	Her lover is with <u>another woman</u> and they think she's <u>at church</u> crying — but she's not.
<u>Lines 9-20</u>	She watches the chemist and says how <u>lovely</u> the <u>poisons</u> look. She wants <u>all of them</u>.
<u>Lines 21-24</u>	She plans to <u>poison two other women</u> called Pauline and Elise at the King's Court.
<u>Lines 25-28</u>	She tells the chemist to make the poison <u>brighter</u>, to make her lover's mistress drink it.
<u>Lines 29-32</u>	She says there's <u>not enough</u> poison to kill the mistress — she's too big and strong.
<u>Lines 33-40</u>	Last night, she felt she could <u>kill</u> the mistress by <u>looking</u> at her. She wants her to die <u>painfully</u>.
<u>Lines 41-48</u>	She's so <u>grateful</u> to the chemist she offers to kiss him. Now she's off to <u>use the poison</u>.

Learn About the Three Types of Language

1) <u>VIOLENT LANGUAGE</u> — She's absolutely <u>merciless</u> about taking her revenge. She wants the mistress's death to be <u>horrible</u> and <u>painful</u>, and violent thoughts are never far from her mind.

2) <u>IMAGERY</u> — For all her nastiness, she can be quite <u>eloquent</u> with her descriptions.

3) <u>OBSESSIVE LANGUAGE</u> — She gives up all her <u>wealth</u> and <u>possessions</u> for the poison — <u>nothing else matters</u> to her. She gets very <u>excited</u> when she thinks about revenge.

Remember the Feelings and Attitudes in the Poem

Ice with your poison,
I mean drink?

1) <u>OBSESSION</u> — She's <u>obsessed</u> with the thought of getting <u>revenge</u>.

2) <u>SINGLE-MINDEDNESS</u> — revenge is all that matters to her.

3) <u>IMMORALITY</u> — She knows what she's doing is <u>wrong</u>, but she <u>doesn't care</u>.

> She wants to kill the mistress just to get revenge on her lover for being unfaithful — pretty twisted really.

Think About Your Feelings and Attitudes to the Poem

1) Pick 2 words or phrases that <u>stand out to you</u>. If none stand out, just pick 2 <u>unusual words or phrases</u>.

2) Write these 2 words or phrases down. Then write about how they <u>make you feel</u>. If they don't make you feel anything, don't worry — just <u>make something up</u>, as long as it's not too stupid.

> **EXAMPLE** I am horrified by the line "He is sure to remember her dying face!". She wants her lover to see his mistress when she dies, which is a very sick way of getting revenge on him.

Themes — evil, danger, characters...

Compare 'The Laboratory' with other poems on the same themes: <u>evil</u> ('Education for Leisure' p.48-49), <u>danger</u> ('Hitcher' p.66-67) and <u>characters</u> ('Havisham' p.36-37, 'Salome' p.42-43 and 'Those bastards in their mansions' p.62-63).

Gerard Manley Hopkins

Gerard Manley Hopkins (1844-1889) was born in Stratford, Essex. He studied Classics at Balliol College, Oxford, and was a famous Victorian poet. He became a Jesuit priest and concentrated on teaching and preaching for several years, before resuming his writing.

Inversnaid

Repetition of how dark the stream is.

Alliteration of "c" sounds makes the stream sound rough.

The water sounds melodic.

This darksome burn, horseback brown,
His rollrock highroad roaring down,
In coop and in comb the fleece of his foam
Flutes and low to the lake falls home.

Alliteration of "r" sounds reminds us of the roar of water.

The bubbles of the stream are described like they're a person's or animal's hair.

Continual motion, like a whirlpool.

5   A windpuff-bonnet of fawn-froth
Turns and twindles over the broth
Of a pool so pitchblack, fell-frowning,
It rounds and rounds Despair to drowning.

The froth is like a hat on the water.

Hostile and unwelcoming.

Alliteration and repetition shows that there's dew all around.

The tree is motionless but alive.

Degged with dew, dappled with dew
10   Are the groins of the braes that the brook treads through,
Wiry heathpacks, flitches of fern,
And the beadbonny ash that sits over the burn.   .

The stream moves like a person walking.

Uses a rhetorical question to appeal to the reader's emotions.

What would the world be, once bereft
Of wet and of wildness? Let them be left,
15   O let them be left, wildness and wet;
Long live the weeds and the wilderness yet.

Repetition creates a passionate, emotional feel.

"W" sounds are repeated throughout this verse.

POEM DICTIONARY
burn — stream
coop — an enclosed area
comb — the top of a wave
fawn — light greyish-brown colour
fell — fiercely
degged — sprinkled
braes — hills
flitches — cuttings
bereft — deprived

Inversnaid

This poem is about a burn (stream) flowing through a rugged, unspoilt area of Scotland.
The area is <u>wild</u> and <u>beautiful</u>, and the poet wants it to stay that way. Don't we all, Gerard...

You've Got to Know What Happens in the Poem

<u>Lines 1-4</u>   A dark-coloured <u>stream</u> flows down into a lake.

<u>Lines 5-8</u>   The stream sounds <u>dark</u> and <u>angry</u>.

<u>Lines 9-12</u>   There's <u>dew</u> on the hills, some <u>wild plants</u>, and an <u>ash tree</u> by the river.

<u>Lines 13-16</u>   The poet says we should <u>leave</u> beautiful places like this <u>as they are</u>.

Learn About the Three Types of Language

1) <u>SOUND EFFECTS</u> — There's loads of <u>alliteration</u> to create the effect of the fast flow of water.
    There's also plenty of <u>rhyming</u>, <u>assonance</u> and <u>onomatopoeia</u> (see glossary, p.92) to help us feel
    like we can really hear the sounds of the country. These effects add to the rugged, natural feel.

2) <u>PERSONIFICATION</u> — The burn is described as if it's a <u>person</u>. This allows the poet
    to make it sound angry and fierce, and also <u>strong</u> and <u>admirable</u>.

3) <u>EMOTIONAL LANGUAGE</u> — The poet feels <u>passionately</u> that places like this should be left alone.
    He seems to be <u>worried</u> that the growth of towns and cities means there are <u>fewer and fewer</u>
    unspoilt areas of countryside.

Remember the Feelings and Attitudes in the Poem

Something's not right...

1) <u>DANGER</u> — The stream seems <u>fierce</u> and <u>dangerous</u>.

2) <u>BEAUTY</u> — The whole area is <u>beautiful</u>, <u>rugged</u> and <u>unspoilt</u>.

3) <u>PRESERVATION</u> — The poet wants this place to stay as it is.
    He believes it would be <u>terrible</u> if beautiful, natural places like
    this <u>didn't exist</u> anymore.

Think About Your Feelings and Attitudes to the Poem

1) Pick 2 words or phrases that <u>stand out to you</u>. If none stand out, just pick 2 <u>unusual words or phrases</u>.

2) Write these 2 words or phrases down. Then write about how they <u>make you feel</u>. If they don't make
    you feel anything, don't worry — just <u>make something up</u>, as long as it's not too stupid.

> **EXAMPLE** When the poet asks "What would the world be, once bereft / Of wet and wildness?",
> it makes me sad. I live in a city, a long way from anywhere like the place the poet describes,
> and I think it is a pity that so many people grow up without knowing places like this.

Themes — imagery, mood, language effects...

Compare this poem with other poems on the same themes: <u>imagery</u> ('Sonnet' p.34-35 and
'Homecoming' p.56-57), <u>mood</u> ('Elvis's Twin Sister' p.38-39 and 'November' p.58-59) and
<u>language effects</u> ('Sonnet 130' p.20-21 and 'Stealing' p.50-51).

John Clare

John Clare (1793-1864) was the son of a Northampton labourer. He left school at 11 and educated himself after that. For most of his life he lived in rural Northamptonshire. He is famous for writing poems about life in the country, although he also wrote about politics, the environment, corruption and poverty.

Repetition emphasises his feelings.	The whole scene is shining brightly.
The colour of wool suggests the purity and cleanliness of the soft, fluffy clouds.	Using "gold" instead of yellow is an idealistic way of seeing it.
Yellow and white enforce the brightness of early summer.	Suggests there's a light, pleasant breeze.
Trees around the lake make it seem alive and healthy.	Rhyming couplets throughout the poem.
Natural and unspoilt.	Gentle movement.
The insects are playful and fun-loving.	Brightness continues to the end of the poem.
Alliteration enforces the idea of brightness.	The poem finishes on a light-hearted, carefree note.

Sonnet

I love to see the summer beaming forth
And white wool sack clouds sailing to the north
I love to see the wild flowers come again
And Mare blobs stain with gold the meadow drain
5 And water lilies whiten on the floods
Where reed clumps rustle like a wind shook wood
Where from her hiding place the Moor Hen pushes
And seeks her flag nest floating in bull rushes
I like the willow leaning half way o'er
10 The clear deep lake to stand upon its shore
I love the hay grass when the flower head swings
To summer winds and insects happy wings
That sport about the meadow the bright day
And see bright beetles in the clear lake play

POEM DICTIONARY
sonnet — a poem with 14 lines
Mare blobs — buttercups
Moor Hen — a bird that lives on ponds
flag — type of leaf
bull rushes — plants that grow in ponds
o'er — over

Sonnet

This is a good old-fashioned poem about how lovely <u>summer</u> in the countryside is. It's a really <u>idealistic</u> poem — the poet talks about all the <u>best</u> things in summer, like pretty flowers, trees and meadows (and ignores things like hayfever and another dull series of Big Brother).

You've Got to Know What Happens in the Poem

<u>Lines 1-4</u>   The poet describes how much he likes the <u>lovely summer</u>, with the <u>lovely clouds</u> floating over the <u>lovely flowers</u> in the <u>lovely meadow</u>.

<u>Lines 5-10</u>   Lilies and reeds grow in the <u>lake</u>. A bird swims across the water. The poet says how great the <u>willow trees</u> on the banks are.

<u>Lines 11-14</u>   He says he loves the way the <u>grass</u> and <u>flowers</u> blow in the <u>wind</u>, and cheery little <u>insects</u> skip about on the surface of the lake.

Learn About the Two Types of Language

1) <u>VISUAL LANGUAGE</u> — <u>Nature</u> is in full bloom. The <u>sun</u> is out, the fields are <u>golden</u> — even the <u>beetles</u> are bright...

2) <u>PEACEFULNESS</u> — The countryside is quiet and calm. The <u>flowers</u> are swaying in the gentle breeze. The insects are just messing around and <u>not stinging</u> anyone. It's a very <u>idealistic</u> poem.

> There's <u>no punctuation</u> in the poem. This helps the poet to create one big image, made up of all the different things he describes.

Remember the Feelings and Attitudes in the Poem

Ah, the glorious British summer of 2004.

1) <u>LOVE</u> — He <u>loves</u> the summer and the natural scenery.
2) <u>TRANQUILLITY</u> — He feels <u>relaxed</u> and <u>at peace</u>.
3) <u>HAPPINESS</u> — Overall, he's just dead <u>happy</u> that it's summer and he's in the countryside. Bless.

Think About Your Feelings and Attitudes to the Poem

1) Pick 2 words or phrases that <u>stand out to you</u>. If none stand out, just pick 2 <u>unusual words or phrases</u>.

2) Write these 2 words or phrases down. Then write about how they <u>make you feel</u>. If they don't make you feel anything, don't worry — just <u>make something up</u>, as long as it's not too stupid.

> **EXAMPLE** The phrase "summer beaming forth" reminds me of the long summer holidays when I was really young. The whole world seemed to be bright and blooming, and this poem brings back the happy, relaxed feelings of that time for me.

Themes — language effects, mood, imagery...

You could compare 'Sonnet' with other poems on the same themes: <u>language effects</u> ('The Eagle' p.24-25 and 'Anne Hathaway' p.40-41), <u>mood</u> ('Inversnaid' p.32-33) and <u>imagery</u> ('Before You Were Mine' p.44-45 and 'My father thought it bloody queer' p.54-55).

Havisham

Carol Ann Duffy was born in 1955 in Glasgow. She studied philosophy at the University of Liverpool, and in 1996 began lecturing in poetry at Manchester Metropolitan University. As well as writing poetry, she has also written plays.

Havisham

Beloved sweetheart bastard. Not a day since then
I haven't wished him dead. Prayed for it
so hard I've dark green pebbles for eyes,
ropes on the back of my hands I could strangle with.

5   Spinster. I stink and remember. Whole days
in bed cawing Nooooo at the wall; the dress
yellowing, trembling if I open the wardrobe;
the slewed mirror, full-length, her, myself, who did this

to me? Puce curses that are sounds not words.
10 Some nights better, the lost body over me,
my fluent tongue in its mouth in its ear
then down till I suddenly bite awake. Love's

hate behind a white veil; a red balloon bursting
in my face. Bang. I stabbed at a wedding-cake.
15 Give me a male corpse for a long slow honeymoon.
Don't think it's only the heart that b-b-b-breaks.

Annotations:

- Her feelings are a confused mix — the tender love she would have had for him as a husband, and her violent bitterness at being rejected.
- She's become so hardened by her hatred that she can't see clearly.
- She's so angry she could use her veins to strangle him.
- She's disgusted with herself too.
- She becomes more reflective here, wondering how she's become so messed up.
- She screams like an animal.
- This shows us how long she's been wearing it.
- She recognises how irrational and savage she's become.
- Even her dreams end violently.
- In her fantasies, the man is seen as an object, not a person.
- The veil usually hides a blushing bride, but here it masks her hatred.
- Could be a sign of a wedding party — a metaphor for her dreams of married bliss being cruelly dashed.
- Any man will do — she wants revenge on men in general.
- Usually a happy time, but here it's connected with death and revenge.
- Could mean that her mind has also broken, or that she wants to break the entire body of a man.

POEM DICTIONARY
spinster — a woman who's never married
cawing — making the sound of a crow
slewed — twisted sideways, lopsided
puce — a deep red or purple colour
fluent — flowing or speaking smoothly

Havisham

Miss Havisham was a character in "Great Expectations" by Charles Dickens. She was jilted on her wedding day and ended up a bit mad, staying in her wedding dress for years with the rotting cake in her room. In this poem, Duffy describes her feelings. It's a tad bitter and twisted, this one...

You've Got to Know What Happens in the Poem

Lines 1-4	Havisham's dead angry. She wants to kill the man who jilted her.
Lines 5-9	She describes the weird things she does — like staying in bed all day screaming, and always wearing her old, manky wedding dress.
Lines 9-12	She says she sometimes dreams there's a man in bed with her, then wakes up abruptly.
Lines 12-16	She tells us that she stabbed the cake, but really wants to stab a man.

Learn About the Three Types of Language

1) **VIOLENT LANGUAGE** — Havisham's hell-bent on revenge. She wants to take out her anger on a man — but settles for stabbing the wedding-cake instead.

2) **REFLECTIVE LANGUAGE** — There are signs that she hasn't always been a nutter. At times she reflects on how she's become like she is, and we see a more sensitive side to her.

3) **WEDDING-RELATED LANGUAGE** — There are plenty of images of weddings — but instead of being signs of love and happiness, they come to stand for Havisham's bitterness and violent streak.

Remember the Feelings and Attitudes in the Poem

"I could murder a slice of cake..."

1) **ANGER** — Havisham is really really really really angry — at the man who jilted her, and also at men in general.

2) **BITTERNESS** — She's very very very bitter about it too. She wants to get revenge.

3) **SADNESS** — She's also unhappy — she uses her violent feelings to cover up the fact that she's actually very upset and vulnerable because she was dumped on her big day.

> Havisham is totally obsessed by what's happened to her. She can't think about anything else, even though it happened years ago.

Think About Your Feelings and Attitudes to the Poem

1) Pick 2 words or phrases that stand out to you. If none stand out, just pick 2 unusual words or phrases.

2) Write these 2 words or phrases down. Then write about how they make you feel. If they don't make you feel anything, don't worry — just make something up, as long as it's not too stupid.

> **EXAMPLE** When Havisham describes herself "trembling if I open the wardrobe", I feel sorry for her. She's so scared of what she has become that she can't even bear to look at herself in the mirror.

Themes — mood, strong emotions and the first person...

Compare 'Havisham' with other poems about the same themes: mood ('Tichborne's Elegy p.14-15), strong emotions ('Those bastards in their mansions' p.62-63 and 'The Affliction of Margaret' p.10-11) and use of the first person ('Kid' p.60-61 and 'Ulysses' p.26-27).

Elvis's Twin Sister

Elvis's Twin Sister

Are you lonesome tonight? Do you miss me tonight?

Elvis is alive and she's female: Madonna

She leads a simple, peaceful life.

In the convent, y'all,
I tend the gardens,
watch things grow,
pray for the immortal soul
5   of rock 'n' roll.

This colloquial greeting reveals her background. She's from the southern USA, like her brother.

Sounds like a typical religious activity, but the next line makes the link with Elvis.

This name combines both aspects of her personality.

They call me
Sister Presley here.
The Reverend Mother
digs the way I move my hips
10   just like my brother.

Humorous image of Elvis's sexy movements in a convent. The use of the slang word "digs" also seems comically out of place.

Peaceful religious singing contrasts with Elvis's rock 'n' roll.

Gregorian chant
drifts out across the herbs
Pascha nostrum immolatus est ...
I wear a simple habit,
15   darkish hues,

A hymn sung at Easter — religion is central to her life.

She has the usual basic clothes and possessions of a nun. They're functional, not fashionable.

a wimple with a novice-sewn
lace band, a rosary,
a chain of keys,
a pair of good and sturdy
20   blue suede shoes.

A similarity with her brother — but she wears them because they're practical, rather than because they're fashionable.

She loves the convent as Elvis loved his home — but maybe the name is more appropriate here, as she's found happiness.

I think of it
as Graceland here,
a land of grace.
It puts my trademark slow lopsided smile
25   back on my face.

Another famous Elvis characteristic — but his sister's smile is genuine, not just a trademark.

Slang way of saying "lord" humorously links the religious and rock 'n' roll parts of her background.

Lawdy.
I'm alive and well.
Long time since I walked
down Lonely Street
30   towards Heartbreak Hotel.

This refers to the rumours that "Elvis lives".

Places from Elvis songs. Heartbreak and loneliness are things of the past now.

POEM DICTIONARY
convent — a place where nuns live
Gregorian chant — a religious style of singing in harmony
habit — a dress worn by a nun
hues — shades, colours

wimple — a piece of cloth that a nun wears around her head
rosary — religious beads
Graceland — the home of Elvis Presley

Section Two — Carol Ann Duffy

Elvis's Twin Sister

The poet imagines that <u>Elvis Presley</u> has a twin sister who's living as a <u>nun</u> (in real life Elvis didn't have a sister). She's happier than her brother was, suggesting that a <u>simple life</u> will bring you more happiness than wealth and fame can bring. If only we could persuade Will Young to be a monk...

You've Got to Know What Happens in the Poem

<u>Lines 1-10</u>   Elvis's imaginary sister talks about her simple, <u>peaceful life</u> as a nun.
          She hints at her similarity in appearance to Elvis (lines 8-10).

<u>Lines 11-20</u>   She describes the religious <u>singing</u> that rings out around the convent.
          She says she wears simple, practical <u>clothes</u>.

<u>Lines 21-30</u>   She's really <u>happy</u> at the convent — she's left her sadness behind.

Learn About the Three Types of Language

1) <u>ELVIS REFERENCES</u> — Lots of famous aspects of Elvis's life (like his <u>songs</u>, <u>looks</u> and <u>clothes</u>) are used to reinforce the idea that the nun is just like him — she's just chosen a <u>different way of life</u>.

2) <u>RELIGIOUS LANGUAGE</u> — The <u>simple clothes</u> and <u>religious lifestyle</u> of the nuns contrast with the flamboyant life that Elvis led. This emphasises the <u>differences</u> between the choices they have made.

3) <u>HUMOUR</u> — The idea of a <u>nun</u> looking and acting <u>like Elvis</u> is pretty funny when you think about it. It adds a light-hearted touch to the poem.

Remember the Feelings and Attitudes in the Poem

1) <u>CONTENTMENT</u> — Elvis's sister is <u>happy</u> living her simple life.

2) <u>HUMOUR</u> — There's a <u>light-hearted</u> feel to the poem — the idea of a nun looking and acting like Elvis is quite <u>comical</u>.

3) <u>SIMPLICITY</u> — The poet could be suggesting that you'll be <u>happier</u> if you lead a <u>simple life</u> than if you go after fame and money.

Think About Your Feelings and Attitudes to the Poem

1) Pick 2 words or phrases that <u>stand out to you</u>. If none stand out, just pick 2 <u>unusual words or phrases</u>.

2) Write these 2 words or phrases down. Then write about how they <u>make you feel</u>. If they don't make you feel anything, don't worry — just <u>make something up</u>, as long as it's not too stupid.

> **EXAMPLE** When Elvis's sister says "The Reverend Mother / digs the way I move my hips", it makes me laugh. The idea of a nun moving like Elvis is comical in itself, but by using the word "digs", Duffy makes it sound like the Reverend Mother is attracted to Elvis's sister just like a fan might be attracted to Elvis. This is funny because nuns are supposed to be well-behaved and more serious than that.

Themes — characters, the first person and imagery...

Compare 'Elvis's Twin Sister' with other poems about the same themes: strong <u>characters</u> ('Salome' p.42-43 and 'My Last Duchess' p.22-23), use of the <u>first person</u> ('My father thought it bloody queer' p.54-55 and 'The Song of the Old Mother' p.8-9) and <u>imagery</u> ('Kid' p.60-61 and 'Sonnet' p.34-35).

Anne Hathaway

Anne Hathaway

'Item I gyve unto my wife my second best bed ...'

(from Shakespeare's will)

> This is how she remembers it, rather than the "second best bed".

> She feels that he took her to romantic, exciting places — it's like being in a fairytale.

> Shows their love was rare and magical.

> She feels they existed in his imagination — their life was a fantasy.

> Other people speak in boring prose — not beautiful poetry like Shakespeare.

> She felt safe and secure with him.

> Her experiences with Shakespeare were everything to her.

> She sees their love as a hidden treasure.

> Their bodies fit together, like a rhyming couplet.

> He injected life and movement into her.

> She feels like she's become part of a work of fiction.

> Sounds ordinary and dull, contrasting with what happened in Anne's bed.

> Alliteration.

> His resting place is inside her head.

> This seems ironic now — it doesn't feel second best to Anne.

The bed we loved in was a spinning world
of forests, castles, torchlight, clifftops, seas
where he would dive for pearls. My lover's words
were shooting stars which fell to earth as kisses
on these lips; my body now a softer rhyme   5
to his, now echo, assonance; his touch
a verb dancing in the centre of a noun.
Some nights, I dreamed he'd written me, the bed
a page beneath his writer's hands. Romance
and drama played by touch, by scent, by taste.   10
In the other bed, the best, our guests dozed on,
dribbling their prose. My living laughing love –
I hold him in the casket of my widow's head
as he held me upon that next best bed.

POEM DICTIONARY
prose — normal writing or speech (not poetry)
casket — coffin

Anne Hathaway

In this poem, Duffy writes as <u>Shakespeare's wife</u>, Anne Hathaway. Like many love poems written by Shakespeare himself, it's a <u>sonnet</u> — a kind of poem with 14 lines. The poem's about what went on in the "second best bed" that Shakespeare left Anne in his will.

You've Got to Know What Happens in the Poem

<u>Lines 1-7</u>	Anne describes her memories of the <u>bed</u>. She associates it with fond memories of her <u>passionate love</u> with Shakespeare. She compares his love to the words in his <u>poems</u>.
<u>Lines 8-10</u>	She seems to see their love as one of Shakespeare's <u>plays</u>.
<u>Lines 11-14</u>	Their guests' time in the better bed seems <u>inferior</u> to the love between Anne and Shakespeare. She says she'll always <u>remember</u> the love between them in that bed (lines 13-14).

Learn About the Two Types of Language

1) <u>ROMANTIC LANGUAGE</u> — There are some quite <u>traditional</u> romantic metaphors. This shows how <u>precious</u> and <u>amazing</u> Anne's time with Shakespeare was. Some of Anne's language reminds us of Shakespeare's own <u>poetry</u>, or <u>speeches</u> from his plays.

2) <u>REFERENCES TO PLAYS AND POEMS</u> — She compares the way Shakespeare loved her to his <u>writing methods</u>. Poetic techniques like <u>rhyming</u> and <u>assonance</u> are mentioned. Their love was so intense that it seemed <u>poetic</u> — Anne felt like she was in a <u>play</u>, rather than the real world.

Remember the Feelings and Attitudes in the Poem

1) <u>FONDNESS</u> — Anne has <u>fond memories</u> of Shakespeare.
2) <u>EXCITEMENT</u> — She's <u>excited</u> just remembering what it was like being with him.
3) <u>FANTASY</u> — She feels like they were in their <u>own world</u>, where everything seemed magical, like a <u>fantasy</u>.

Think About Your Feelings and Attitudes to the Poem

1) Pick 2 words or phrases that <u>stand out to you</u>. If none stand out, just pick 2 <u>unusual words or phrases</u>.
2) Write these 2 words or phrases down. Then write about how they <u>make you feel</u>. If they don't make you feel anything, don't worry — just <u>make something up</u>, as long as it's not too stupid.

> **EXAMPLE** I think it's really beautiful when Anne says "My lover's words / were shooting stars". It reminds me of how excited I feel when I read my boyfriend's love letters.

Themes — love, memory and closing couplets...

Compare 'Anne Hathaway' with other poems about the same themes: <u>love</u> ('Mother, any distance...' p.52-53 and 'On my first Sonne' p.6-7), <u>memory</u> ('We Remember Your Childhood Well' p.46-47 and 'My Last Duchess' p.22-23) and a <u>closing couplet</u> ('Sonnet 130' p.20-21).

Salome

Salome

She's only slightly regretful — which is shocking when we realise what she's actually done.

Black humour — she doesn't tell us that there isn't a body attached to the head.

I'd done it before
(and doubtless I'll do it again,
sooner or later)
woke up with a head on the pillow beside me – whose? –
5   what did it matter?

Sounds like she's having a light-hearted chat with a friend.

The pain is more recent than we realise.

Good-looking, of course, dark hair, rather matted;
the reddish beard several shades lighter;
with very deep lines around the eyes,
from pain, I'd guess, maybe laughter;
10   and a beautiful crimson mouth that obviously knew
how to flatter ...
which I kissed ...
Colder than pewter.
Strange. What was his name? Peter?

At first we think this means his hair is thick or tangled — but it could actually be matted with blood.

Sounds natural and normal here — but the colouring is really from blood stains.

The coldness hints at what we find out later — he's dead.

15   Simon? Andrew? John? I knew I'd feel better
for tea, dry toast, no butter,
so rang for the maid.
And, indeed, her innocent clatter
of cups and plates,
20   her clearing of clutter,
her regional patter,
were just what needed –
hungover and wrecked as I was from a night on the batter.

Biblical names suggest the link with Salome.

Suggests she's well-off.

Rhyming, here and in other verses, makes her sound in control — she didn't do it by accident.

We think this means she's been drinking. But it turns out to have a more literal, violent meaning.

She complains about minor problems like being hungover, but doesn't seem bothered about the man she's killed.

Never again!
25   I needed to clean up my act,
get fitter,
cut out the booze and the fags and the sex.
Yes. And as for the latter,
it was time to turf out the blighter,
30   the beater or biter,
who'd come like a lamb to the slaughter
to Salome's bed.

Common, everyday sayings suggest she's a normal person with normal problems.

Light-hearted expression.

Christian image of innocence which contrasts with the previous line — now he's the victim.

Without knowing who he is, she assumes he's violent.

She makes her connection to Salome clear — we expect the worst now.

In the mirror, I saw my eyes glitter.
I flung back the sticky red sheets,
35   and there, like I said – and ain't life a bitch –
was his head on a platter.

An evil look before she reveals the truth.

Sarcastically pretends to be bothered — she doesn't seem to really care about what she's done.

The poem finishes with a shocking revelation. But even here, her tone is calm.

POEM DICTIONARY
Salome — Biblical woman who tricked Herod into giving her the head of John the Baptist on a plate
crimson — a deep red colour
pewter — a kind of metal, made up mainly of tin
platter — a large dish for food

Salome

This poem's pretty grim. The woman in the poem wakes up after a <u>one-night stand</u>, after getting drunk the night before. She regrets it and says she needs to stop doing this sort of thing. Then it turns out she's <u>cut the bloke's head off</u>. Nice.

You've Got to Know What Happens in the Poem

<u>Lines 1-14</u>   The character in the poem wakes up with a <u>man's head</u> on the pillow next to her. She <u>can't remember</u> who he is.

<u>Lines 15-23</u>   She calls for her <u>maid</u>, who enters making loads of <u>noise</u>.

<u>Lines 24-32</u>   She says she needs to <u>cut out</u> her unhealthy habits and <u>get rid</u> of the man in her bed.

<u>Lines 33-36</u>   She pulls the sheets back, and we realise there's nothing there but his <u>severed head</u>.

Learn About the Three Types of Language

1) <u>DOUBLE MEANINGS</u> — Some of the language in the poem can be read in a <u>different way</u> after finding out that she's actually <u>killed</u> the man, rather than just sleeping with him. There's some <u>black humour</u> in the double meanings — they're both <u>horrible and funny</u> at the same time.

2) <u>CASUAL LANGUAGE</u> — The woman describes the incident as if it's just a <u>normal event</u>. Her <u>casual tone</u> is really <u>shocking</u> when we realise the full horror of what she'd done.

3) <u>BIBLICAL REFERENCES</u> — The poem is set in the <u>modern day</u>, but there are references to <u>religious stories</u> which connect what happens to the story of <u>Salome</u>.

Remember the Feelings and Attitudes in the Poem

"More blood, ma'am?"

1) <u>CASUALNESS</u> — At first, the woman seems vaguely <u>regretful</u> — but we soon start to realise that she's <u>not all that bothered</u>.

2) <u>NASTINESS</u> — We see her <u>evil</u> side at the end of the poem.

3) <u>PRIDE</u> — She even seems quite <u>proud</u> of killing the man — she seems to <u>enjoy</u> letting us think she's only slept with him, before dramatically revealing the truth at the end of the poem.

Think About Your Feelings and Attitudes to the Poem

1) Pick 2 words or phrases that <u>stand out to you</u>. If none stand out, just pick 2 <u>unusual words or phrases</u>.

2) Write these 2 words or phrases down. Then write about how they <u>make you feel</u>. If they don't make you feel anything, don't worry — just <u>make something up</u>, as long as it's not too stupid.

> **EXAMPLE** The line "I flung back the sticky red sheets" makes me feel sick. I find it disgusting that she could be lying there in a bed drenched in blood, talking calmly about chopping off a man's head.

Themes — evil, irony and characters...

Compare 'Salome' with other poems about the same themes: <u>evil</u> ('Hitcher' p.66-67 and 'The Last Duchess' p.22-23), <u>irony</u> ('Tichborne's Elegy' p.14-15 and 'The Man He Killed' p.16-17), and <u>character</u> ('Havisham' p.36-37 and 'The Laboratory' p.30-31).

Key Poem

Before You Were Mine

The first 3 verses each start with a reminder of the distance in time between the poet's birth and her mum's youth and fun.

The poet talks directly to her mum.

Before You Were Mine

I'm ten years away from the corner you laugh on
with your pals, Maggie McGeeney and Jean Duff.
The three of you bend from the waist, holding
each other, or your knees, and shriek at the pavement.
5 Your polka-dot dress blows round your legs. Marilyn.

Her mother's life was fun before she was born.

Compares her mother with Marilyn Monroe — she was glamorous and desirable.

There could be a hint of jealousy here.

Her mum was the centre of attention, with exciting opportunities.

I'm not here yet. The thought of me doesn't occur
in the ballroom with the thousand eyes, the fizzy, movie tomorrows
the right walk home could bring. I knew you would dance
like that. Before you were mine, your Ma stands at the close
10 with a hiding for the late one. You reckon it's worth it.

She used to belong to herself, not someone else.

Her mum was wasn't scared of the consequences of enjoying herself.

The poet was a demanding baby.

The decade ahead of my loud, possessive yell was the best one, eh?
I remember my hands in those high-heeled red shoes, relics,
and now your ghost clatters toward me over George Square
till I see you, clear as scent, under the tree,
15 with its lights, and whose small bites on your neck, sweetheart?

The glamour is a thing of the past, and won't return.

Sounds like something a parent would say to their child, but here it's the other way around.

Alliteration stresses her mum's defiance and energy.

Cha cha cha! You'd teach me the steps on the way home from Mass,
stamping stars from the wrong pavement. Even then
I wanted the bold girl winking in Portobello, somewhere
in Scotland, before I was born. That glamorous love lasts
20 where you sparkle and waltz and laugh before you were mine.

Contrasts with "the right walk home" (line 8). Maybe she's made the wrong choice in life.

Repeating this emphasises the difference between then and now.

Emphasises that the poet's birth was the turning point in her mum's life.

She was bright, energetic and fun-loving.

As a child, the poet wanted what she couldn't have — her birth meant that her mum couldn't be a "bold girl" any more.

Before You Were Mine

The poet talks to her mother about the ten years before the poet's birth. She imagines her mum led a fun-filled, <u>carefree</u> life. But that all changed when she became a mother, and her child took her <u>freedom</u> away. The poet wants the happy, fun-loving girl, but realises she only exists in the past.

You've Got to Know What Happens in the Poem

<u>Lines 1-5</u>	The poet describes her mum having fun with <u>friends</u>. She compares her with <u>Marilyn Monroe</u>.
<u>Lines 6-11</u>	Her mum stayed out late <u>dancing</u>, not put off by being <u>told off</u> by her own mother. The poet says that her mother was <u>happiest</u> during the ten years before she was born.
<u>Lines 12-15</u>	The poet remembers <u>glimpses</u> of her mum's fun-loving past from when she was a <u>child</u>.
<u>Lines 16-20</u>	She remembers her mum teaching her to <u>dance</u>. She wanted her to be like this more often, but realises that she was only really fun-loving and glamorous <u>before</u> she was born.

Learn About the Three Types of Language

1) <u>EXCITING LANGUAGE</u> — There are loads of words and phrases which describe how <u>exciting</u>, <u>fun</u> and <u>glamorous</u> the poet's mum's life was before the poet was born.

2) <u>POSSESSIVE LANGUAGE</u> — It seems that when the poet was born, she <u>took control</u> of her mum, and her mum couldn't be <u>free</u> any more. The idea of <u>breaking free</u> from your parents is turned on its head, with the child stopping the parent from having fun.

3) <u>LANGUAGE ABOUT TIME</u> — There's a very clear <u>division</u> between the time <u>before</u> the poet was born and the time <u>after</u> she was born, when her mum's glamorous life came to an <u>abrupt end</u>.

Remember the Feelings and Attitudes in the Poem

Not to be confused with Marilyn Manson.

1) <u>ADMIRATION</u> — The poet <u>admires</u> her mum's headstrong, rebellious approach to life.

2) <u>NOSTALGIA</u> — She wishes her mum was <u>still fun-loving</u> and carefree.

3) <u>SELF-CRITICISM</u> — The poet seems to <u>criticise</u> herself for taking away her mum's freedom (line 11).

Think About Your Feelings and Attitudes to the Poem

1) Pick 2 words or phrases that <u>stand out to you</u>. If none stand out, just pick 2 <u>unusual words or phrases</u>.

2) Write these 2 words or phrases down. Then write about how they <u>make you feel</u>. If they don't make you feel anything, don't worry — just <u>make something up</u>, as long as it's not too stupid.

> **EXAMPLE** When the poet says "I wanted the bold girl winking in Portobello", it makes me sad. She seems to admire the happy, rebellious side of her mother more than the responsible parent side, but the poet knows that she is the very reason for the change in her mother's lifestyle.

Themes — parent/child, getting older, imagery...

Compare 'Before You Were Mine' with other poems about the same themes: <u>parent/child relationships</u> ('My father thought it bloody queer' p.54-55), <u>getting older</u> ('Mother, any distance' p.52-53) and <u>imagery</u> ('Homecoming' p.56-57 and 'Kid' p.60-61).

We Remember Your Childhood Well

The poem starts on a defensive note. We know they wouldn't say this if there hadn't been an accusation.

The memories are entirely negative.

We Remember Your Childhood Well

Nobody hurt you. Nobody turned off the light and argued
with somebody else all night. The bad man on the moors
was only a movie you saw. Nobody locked the door.

Your questions were answered fully. No. That didn't occur.
5   You couldn't sing anyway, cared less. The moment's a blur, a *Film Fun*
laughing itself to death in the coal fire. Anyone's guess.

Nobody forced you. You wanted to go that day. Begged. You chose
the dress. Here are the pictures, look at you. Look at us all,
smiling and waving, younger. The whole thing is inside your head.

10 What you recall are impressions; we have the facts. We called the tune.
The secret police of your childhood were older and wiser than you, bigger
than you. Call back the sound of their voices. Boom. Boom. Boom.

Nobody sent you away. That was an extra holiday, with people
you seemed to like. They were firm, there was nothing to fear.
15 There was none but yourself to blame if it ended in tears.

What does it matter now? No, no, nobody left the skidmarks of sin
on your soul and laid you wide open for Hell. You were loved.
Always. We did what was best. We remember your childhood well.

This refers to the child murders on the Lancashire moors in the 1960s.

Suggests the person was trapped.

They make it as vague as possible, to try to confuse the person and cover up the truth.

They say that it was the child's choice. This seems unlikely as they don't let that person get a word in now.

They use images of happiness to cover up the painful truth.

At least they're honest here — they were in charge.

Sounds sinister and controlling.

The voices were loud and angry.

They even tell the person what their own feelings and opinions were.

The denials now sound very forceful.

Suggests the pain of the person's childhood still affects him/her now.

They shift all the guilt and responsibility onto the child.

The person feels that what happened in their childhood ruined the rest of their life.

They insist that their version of events is more accurate than the person whose childhood is being discussed.

POEM DICTIONARY
Film Fun — a magazine about films

Section Two — Carol Ann Duffy

We Remember Your Childhood Well

In this poem, the people speaking <u>deny</u> that anything <u>bad</u> happened in someone's childhood (possibly their son or daughter). The child seems to have claimed he or she was abused, but we <u>never hear</u> that side of the story, so we can only guess what happened from what the people denying it say.

You've Got to Know What Happens in the Poem

<u>Lines 1-3</u>	The people speaking deny the claim that the person they're speaking to was <u>abused</u> as a child.
<u>Lines 4-6</u>	There are more <u>denials</u>. They say the child was never really bothered about <u>singing</u>.
<u>Lines 7-9</u>	They deny <u>forcing</u> the child to go somewhere. They say the child <u>wanted</u> to go, and enjoyed it.
<u>Lines 10-12</u>	Aggressively, they say that they're the only ones who can remember <u>what really happened</u>.
<u>Lines 13-18</u>	They again <u>deny</u> sending the child away. They tell the child that it was his/her <u>own fault</u> if anything bad happened. They claim they treated the child <u>well</u>.

Learn About the Three Types of Language

1) <u>DENIAL</u> — We don't hear the accusations, but the denials give us <u>clues</u> as to what they are. There's a <u>defensive</u> tone right from the start — we can tell the people speaking are <u>covering something up</u>.

2) <u>AGGRESSION</u> — The tone becomes more <u>threatening</u> as the poem goes on. The people speaking find it more and more difficult to pretend to be pleasant, and in the end resort to <u>threats</u> and <u>guilt trips</u>.

3) <u>PAIN and FEAR</u> — The childhood memories are <u>confused</u> and <u>scary</u>. The fact that we <u>don't find out</u> exactly what happened increases the sense of fear in the poem. Past events seem to have caused <u>lasting pain</u> to the person, even after growing up.

Remember the Feelings and Attitudes in the Poem

1) <u>CRUELTY</u> — There's a <u>cruel</u>, <u>sinister</u> feel to the poem.

2) <u>SUSPICION</u> — We suspect that <u>bad things</u> happened to the child, but the people speaking are trying to <u>cover up</u> the truth.

3) <u>GUILT</u> — They even try to make the <u>victim</u> feel that what happened was his/her <u>fault</u>.

4) <u>PAIN</u> — There's a real sense of <u>pain</u> and <u>sadness</u> — it seems that the person's life has been <u>ruined</u> by the events in his/her childhood (lines 16-17).

Think About Your Feelings and Attitudes to the Poem

1) Pick 2 words or phrases that <u>stand out to you</u>. If none stand out, just pick 2 <u>unusual words or phrases</u>.

2) Write these 2 words or phrases down. Then write about how they <u>make you feel</u>. If they don't make you feel anything, don't worry — just <u>make something up</u>, as long as it's not too stupid.

> **EXAMPLE** When the people in the poem say "There was none but yourself to blame if it ended in tears", I feel angry. Trying to make someone feel guilty for something that happened when they were a child is an extremely cruel thing to do.

Themes — mood, attitudes towards others, memory...

Compare 'We Remember Your Childhood Well' to other poems about the same themes: <u>mood</u> ('Hitcher' p.66-67, 'The Little Boy Lost' and 'The Little Boy Found' p.12-13), <u>attitudes towards other people</u> ('My Last Duchess' p.22-23) and <u>memory</u> ('Homecoming' p.56-57).

Key Poem

Education for Leisure

Education for Leisure

Today I am going to kill something. Anything.
I have had enough of being ignored and today
I am going to play God. It is an ordinary day,
a sort of grey with boredom stirring in the streets.

5   I squash a fly against the window with my thumb.
We did that at school. Shakespeare. It was in
another language and now the fly is in another language.
I breathe out talent on the glass to write my name.

I am a genius. I could be anything at all, with half
10 the chance. But today I am going to change the world.
Something's world. The cat avoids me. The cat
knows I am a genius, and has hidden itself.

I pour the goldfish down the bog. I pull the chain.
I see that it is good. The budgie is panicking.
15 Once a fortnight, I walk the two miles into town
for signing on. They don't appreciate my autograph.

There is nothing left to kill. I dial the radio
and tell the man he's talking to a superstar.
He cuts me off. I get our bread-knife and go out.
20 The pavements glitter suddenly. I touch your arm.

He/she is motivated by the need for attention.

Wants to be grand and powerful.

Not a very impressive achievement.

He/she breathes on the mirror. He/she thinks even this shows talent.

Very arrogant. There's nothing to back this claim up.

He/she blames others for their own failures.

Pathetic and darkly humorous attempt at being powerful.

Sounds Biblical — trying to live up to the intention of playing God.

Sounds disappointed.

More rejection. "Cuts" seems to give the character the idea of getting the knife.

Excitement contrasts with line 4.

Matter-of-fact tone is chilling.

Alliteration adds to the irritable feeling.

He/she felt excluded because they couldn't understand it.

Another boast — but it seems he/she hasn't achieved anything.

This ambitious claim contrasts with what he/she actually does.

Scaring the pets is a comically poor attempt at being powerful.

The character thinks he/she deserves to be recognised.

Suggests the character is famous and popular, but we know this isn't true.

Purposeful, violent tone.

Now he/she threatens the reader.

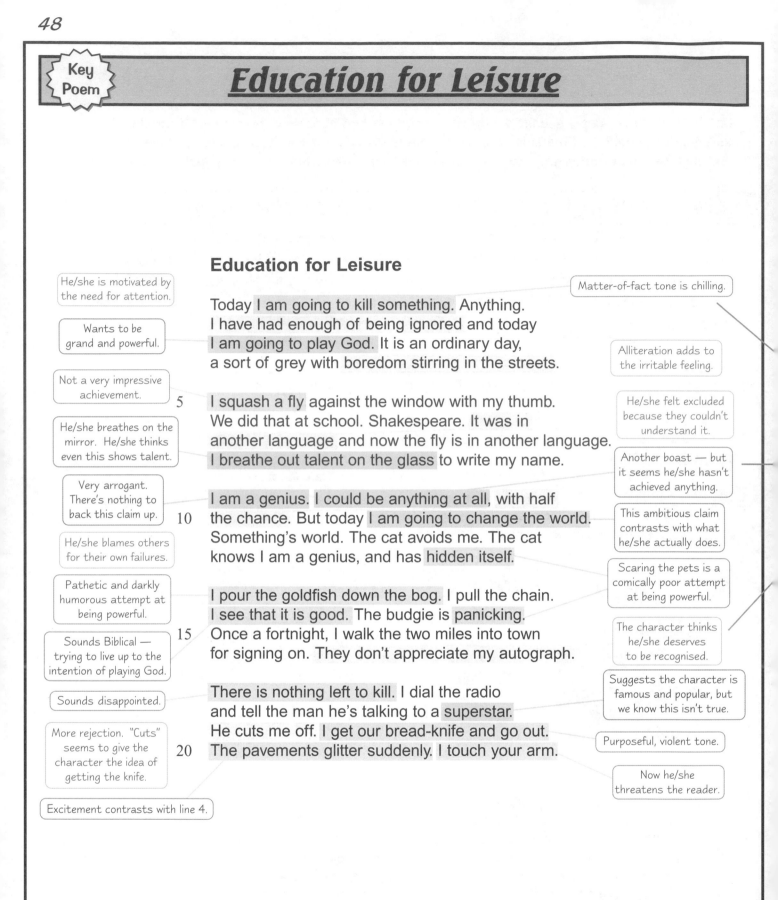

POEM DICTIONARY
signing on — registering for unemployment benefit

Section Two — Carol Ann Duffy

Education for Leisure

The person in this poem is a bit disturbed. Fed up of feeling bored and ignored, he/she goes on a <u>killing spree</u>, starting with animals. Then they go outside with a <u>knife</u>, presumably to kill people, although we don't find out exactly what happens then. I just read a book when I'm bored...

You've Got to Know What Happens in the Poem

<u>Lines 1-4</u>   The character in the poem is <u>bored</u> and <u>restless</u>, so he/she decides to <u>kill something</u>.

<u>Lines 5-7</u>   The character kills a <u>fly</u>, which makes him/her think about how he/she felt <u>excluded</u> at school.

<u>Lines 8-14</u>   The character claims to be a <u>genius</u> and is <u>determined</u> to prove it.
             He/she enjoys the <u>power</u> of <u>killing the pets</u> in the house.

<u>Lines 15-20</u> The character is <u>annoyed</u> that no-one recognises or respects him/her.
             He/she gets a <u>knife</u> and goes outside.

Learn About the Three Types of Language

1) <u>VIOLENT LANGUAGE</u> — The person in the poem kills <u>everything they can find</u> in the house, then goes outside to continue the <u>killing spree</u>. The really shocking thing about the violence is the character's <u>calm tone</u> — as if he/she is describing <u>normal</u> and <u>reasonable</u> behaviour.

2) <u>BOASTFUL LANGUAGE</u> — The character seems really arrogant. Loads of the sentences begin with "I", showing how <u>self-obsessed</u> the character is.

3) <u>LANGUAGE OF REJECTION</u> — The character feels <u>rejected</u> and <u>excluded</u>. He/she wants to be well-known instead of ignored, and the mindless violence is his/her way of trying to be <u>recognised</u>.

Remember the Feelings and Attitudes in the Poem

"Uh-oh..."

1) <u>RESENTMENT</u> — The character <u>resents</u> the way people <u>ignore</u> him/her.

2) <u>GRIM DETERMINATION</u> — He/she is <u>determined</u> to make their mark on the world, by showing how <u>powerful</u> he/she is.

3) <u>CALMNESS</u> — He/she is very <u>laid back</u> about all the killing.

4) <u>ENJOYMENT</u> — He/she <u>enjoys</u> the sense of power they get from killing.

Clearly the character has <u>lost the plot</u> — he/she thinks killing the fish is a sign of genius, and seems ready to kill anyone just to get attention.

Think About Your Feelings and Attitudes to the Poem

1) Pick 2 words or phrases that <u>stand out to you</u>. If none stand out, just pick 2 <u>unusual words or phrases</u>.

2) Write these 2 words or phrases down. Then write about how they <u>make you feel</u>. If they don't make you feel anything, don't worry — just <u>make something up</u>, as long as it's not too stupid.

EXAMPLE When the person in the poem says "I touch your arm", it sends a chill down my spine. At this point it seems that, now he/she has run out of animals to kill, he/she will kill anyone they find, starting with the reader.

Themes — danger, death, the first person...

Compare 'Education for Leisure' with other poems about the same themes: <u>danger</u> ('Stealing' p.50-51 and 'Those bastards in their mansions' p.62-63), <u>death</u> ('Hitcher' p.66-67 and 'The Man He Killed' p.16-17) and use of the first person ('Kid' p.60-61 and 'The Laboratory' p.30-31).

Stealing

Stealing

The most unusual thing I ever stole? A snowman.
Midnight. He looked magnificent; a tall, white mute
beneath the winter moon. I wanted him, a mate
with a mind as cold as the slice of ice
5   within my own brain. I started with the head.

Better off dead than giving in, not taking
what you want. He weighed a ton; his torso,
frozen stiff, hugged to my chest, a fierce chill
piercing my gut. Part of the thrill was knowing
10   that children would cry in the morning. Life's tough.

Sometimes I steal things I don't need. I joy-ride cars
to nowhere, break into houses just to have a look.
I'm a mucky ghost, leave a mess, maybe pinch a camera.
I watch my gloved hand twisting the doorknob.
15   A stranger's bedroom. Mirrors. I sigh like this – *Aah.*

It took some time. Reassembled in the yard,
he didn't look the same. I took a run
and booted him. Again. Again. My breath ripped out
in rags. It seems daft now. Then I was standing
20   alone amongst lumps of snow, sick of the world.

Boredom. Mostly I'm so bored I could eat myself.
One time, I stole a guitar and thought I might
learn to play. I nicked a bust of Shakespeare once,
flogged it, but the snowman was strangest.
25   You don't understand a word I'm saying, do you?

Alliteration creates a sense that the character feels passionate about the snowman.

Suggests he/she feels emotionally frozen.

The split rhyme emphasises excitement as well as the sharp coldness.

This metaphor suggests the narrator spoils things, and also that he/she feels dead like a ghost.

Realises how pointless and silly it sounds.

More slang words.

Realises that he/she isn't making any sense.

It sounds like the character in the poem is responding to a question the reader has asked.

The snowman is unable to communicate, like the character in the poem.

Rhyming makes these 2 words seem connected, suggesting the narrator's dead emotions.

Seems to be boasting here.

Offhand comment — doesn't care about the effects on other people.

Use of slang shows the character's casual approach to theft.

Sounds both threatening and forlorn — the character's life is lonely and unreal.

The character's actions have a violent and destructive result on his/her own body.

Self-destructive and pointless.

POEM DICTIONARY
reassembled — put back together
bust — a statue of someone's head and shoulders

Stealing

The rather strange character in the poem remembers <u>stealing a snowman</u>. Then he/she describes stealing lots of other things because he/she was <u>bored</u>. The dirty tea-leaf.

You've Got to Know What Happens in the Poem

<u>Lines 1-10</u>   The character in the poem remembers stealing a <u>snowman</u> at night, bit by bit.
          This seems to have been for <u>company</u>, and also to make the children who made it cry.

<u>Lines 11-15</u>   The character describes stealing cars, cameras and other things — and getting a <u>thrill</u> from it.

<u>Lines 16-20</u>   The character couldn't put the snowman back together properly — so he/she <u>destroyed</u> it.

<u>Lines 21-25</u>   The character says he/she steals because of <u>boredom</u>, but can't seem to explain it properly.

Learn About the Three Types of Language

1)   <u>CONVERSATIONAL LANGUAGE</u> — It feels like the character is <u>talking directly</u> to us.
     His/her chatty tone of voice shows how <u>casual</u> he/she is about stealing.

2)   <u>SIMILES</u> and <u>METAPHORS</u> — There's also some quite <u>descriptive</u> language, which <u>contrasts</u> with
     the normally down-to-earth tone. It's as if his/her <u>real feelings</u> are struggling to come out.

3)   <u>SOUND EFFECTS</u> — The irregular <u>rhymes</u>, sometimes between words on the same line,
     and <u>alliteration</u> draw the reader's attention to certain combinations of words.

Remember the Feelings and Attitudes in the Poem

1)   <u>ENTHUSIASM</u> — At the start of the poem, the thief is <u>enthusiastic</u>
     about explaining why he/she steals things.

2)   <u>BOREDOM</u> — By the end, <u>loneliness</u> and <u>boredom</u> take over.

3)   <u>FRUSTRATION</u> — He/she is <u>frustrated</u> and <u>angry</u> when destroying the snowman.

4)   <u>FUTILITY</u> — At the end, he/she feels the whole attempt to explain it is <u>futile</u>.

Think About Your Feelings and Attitudes to the Poem

1)   Pick 2 words or phrases that <u>stand out to you</u>. If none stand out, just pick 2 <u>unusual words or phrases</u>.

2)   Write these 2 words or phrases down. Then write about how they <u>make you feel</u>. If they don't make
     you feel anything, don't worry — just <u>make something up</u>, as long as it's not too stupid.

> **EXAMPLE**   The statement "better off dead than giving in, not taking / what you want" makes me
> angry with the person in the poem. He/she is trying to come across as bold and decisive, but this
> sentence really shows how selfish the character is, not thinking about anyone but him/herself.

Themes — attitudes towards others, danger, language...

Compare 'Stealing' with other poems about the same themes: <u>attitudes towards others</u> ('November'
p.58-59 and 'Hitcher' p.66-67), <u>danger</u> ('Education for Leisure' p.48-49 and 'Those bastards in
their mansions' p.62-63) and <u>language effects</u> ('The Laboratory' p.30-31 and 'Kid' p.60-61).

Mother, any distance

Key Poem

Simon Armitage was born in 1963 in Huddersfield, West Yorkshire. As well as poetry, he's also written four stage plays, and writes for TV, film and radio. He studied at Leeds University and he now teaches at Manchester Metropolitan University.

from **Book of Matches**

> Mother, any distance greater than a single span
> requires a second pair of hands.
> You come to help me measure windows, pelmets, doors,
> the acres of the walls, the prairies of the floors.
>
> 5   You at the zero-end, me with the spool of tape, recording
> length, reporting metres, centimetres back to base, then leaving
> up the stairs, the line still feeding out, unreeling
> years between us. Anchor. Kite.
>
> I space-walk through the empty bedrooms, climb
> 10 the ladder to the loft, to breaking point, where something
> has to give;
> two floors below your fingertips still pinch
> the last one-hundredth of an inch ... I reach
> towards a hatch that opens on an endless sky
> 15 to fall or fly.

Annotations:

- He addresses her directly. It's like a personal message to her.
- Holding the start of the tape measure could stand for her thinking back to when he was born.
- He moves upwards and away from his mother.
- They have to let go of their shared history.
- Being on his own is like an adventure on a different planet.
- She's now only a small part of his life.
- Suggests he's "flying the nest". He doesn't know if he'll succeed or fail.
- Double meaning — a "span" is a measurement, but it could also mean "life-span".
- Without his mother, even the walls and floors seem daunting.
- He feels free to fly away. His mother will keep him from getting carried away.
- They have to sever their ties at some point.
- She won't let go completely.
- He feels there's no limit to the opportunities open to him. They can't be measured like the walls.

POEM DICTIONARY
pelmets — boards or material above a window which hide the curtain rail

Mother, any distance

In this poem, the poet is <u>moving out</u> of his mum's house. But he still needs her to help measure things in his new house, and this becomes a metaphor for how he can always <u>turn to her</u> for support if he needs to. Like when his laundry needs doing, probably...

You've Got to Know What Happens in the Poem

Lines 1-4   The poet's <u>mother</u> comes to the house he's moving into, to help <u>measure walls</u> and other things.

Lines 5-8   She holds the <u>end</u> of the tape measure while he walks away to measure things. This makes him think about how she's always <u>looked after him</u> — but now she has to <u>let him go</u>.

Lines 9-15   The poet is <u>looking forward</u> to being independent, but he's also a bit <u>scared</u> by it. He doesn't know if he'll <u>succeed</u> without his mum or not, but she'll <u>always be there</u> for him if he needs her.

Learn About the Two Types of Language

1) **LANGUAGE ABOUT MEASUREMENT** — Measurements and distances are an <u>extended metaphor</u> in this poem. They represent the poet's changing relationship with his <u>mother</u>. They were once <u>close</u>, but they are now becoming more <u>distant</u>.

2) **LANGUAGE ABOUT MOVEMENT** — Walking around his own house is like <u>exploring</u> a new world. He feels ready to "<u>fly</u>" away from his mum (lines 13-15), but she seems ready to <u>catch him</u> when he falls (lines 12-13).

Remember the Feelings and Attitudes in the Poem

1) **EXCITEMENT** — The poet is <u>excited</u> about being independent in his new life.

2) **FEAR** — He's also <u>worried</u> by the thought of being on his own.

3) **ACCEPTANCE** — He <u>accepts</u> that his mother will always be a part of his life.

4) **APPRECIATION** — He seems to <u>appreciate</u> that he can turn to her if he needs her.

Think About Your Feelings and Attitudes to the Poem

1) Pick 2 words or phrases that <u>stand out to you</u>. If none stand out, just pick 2 <u>unusual words or phrases</u>.

2) Write these 2 words or phrases down. Then write about how they <u>make you feel</u>. If they don't make you feel anything, don't worry — just <u>make something up</u>, as long as it's not too stupid.

EXAMPLE When the poet says "I space-walk through the empty bedrooms", I feel both excited and nervous for him. This line shows that breaking free from his mother is a big adventure for him, but also that he is now on his own in the big wide world.

Themes — parent/child relationships, getting older, imagery

Compare 'Mother, any distance...' with other poems about the same themes: <u>parent/child relationships</u> ('Before You Were Mine' p.44-45 and 'The Affliction of Margaret' p.10-11), <u>getting older</u> ('Kid' p.60-61) and <u>imagery</u> ('Anne Hathaway' p.40-41 and 'I've made out a will' p.64-65).

My father thought it bloody queer

from **Book of Matches**

The word "queer" could mean "odd" — but it could also mean his dad thinks the earring looks gay.

Could suggest he was drunk when he got his ear pierced.

Bulls are led around by a nose-ring — his dad says he got the earring because his mates told him to get one.

My father thought it bloody queer,
the day I rolled home with a ring of silver in my ear
half hidden by a mop of hair. 'You've lost your head.
If that's how easily you're led
5   you should've had it through your nose instead.'

His scruffy hair-do shows he's trying to be a rebel.

Could mean either "You've gone mad" or "I can't even see your head any more."

As well as not having the courage to do it, the word "nerve" suggests he couldn't take the pain.

And even then I hadn't had the nerve to numb
the lobe with ice, then drive a needle through the skin,
then wear a safety-pin. It took a jeweller's gun
to pierce the flesh, and then a friend
10   to thread a sleeper in, and where it slept
the hole became a sore, became a wound, and wept.

Sounds violent and painful.

This shows that it bled, and also suggests it made him cry with the pain — not very rebellious.

He's just inflicted an unnecessary injury on himself.

At twenty-nine, it comes as no surprise to hear
my own voice breaking like a tear, released like water,
cried from way back in the spiral of the ear. *If I were you,*
15   *I'd take it out and leave it out next year.*

Remembering his dad's reaction upsets him.

He remembers his voice breaking as a teenager. It's also breaking now, with emotion.

This is a common saying, but here it has a more literal meaning — in a way he <u>has</u> become his father.

It's not entirely clear who he's talking to here. But by saying the same things as his dad, it seems the poet has come to see things the same way his dad did.

This description suggests his emotions being bottled up, then suddenly flooding out.

<u>POEM DICTIONARY</u>
sleeper — a stud to stop a pierced ear from closing up

Section Three — Simon Armitage

My father thought it bloody queer

The poet describes a time when he was a teenager and got his <u>ear pierced</u>. His dad wasn't impressed, and his attempt to be a rebel seemed a bit <u>stupid</u>. Now he's grown up, he hears himself saying the same things his dad said. Now where's my pipe...

You've Got to Know What Happens in the Poem

<u>Lines 1-5</u>   The poet remembers coming home after getting his <u>ear pierced</u>.
           His <u>dad</u> took the mickey out of him and said it was <u>stupid</u>.

<u>Lines 6-11</u> The poet says that he <u>didn't have the courage</u> to pierce his own ear, so he
           got a <u>jeweller</u> to do it. Afterwards, his ear went all sore and <u>bled</u>. Awww...

<u>Lines 12-15</u> Now the poet's <u>grown up</u>, his dad's comments still upset him.
           He says the <u>same things</u> his dad used to say.

Learn About the Three Types of Language

1) <u>DESCRIPTIVE LANGUAGE</u> — The poet's <u>scruffy appearance</u> when he comes home with the earring shows that he's a <u>typical teenager</u>. This makes him seem predictable and conventional — not <u>rebellious</u> as he thought at the time.

2) <u>AMBIGUOUS LANGUAGE</u> — A lot of the words and phrases in this poem are <u>ambiguous</u> — they look like they have <u>one meaning</u>, then when you read them again they mean <u>something else</u>.

3) <u>PAINFUL LANGUAGE</u> — The poet describes two kinds of pain — <u>physical pain</u> from having his ear pierced, and <u>emotional pain</u> when he remembers his dad's reaction and how stupid he felt.

Remember the Feelings and Attitudes in the Poem

"Father, I want to be a doctor."

1) <u>AMUSEMENT</u> — The poet's descriptions of his <u>funny appearance</u> suggest he's <u>amused</u> when he remembers the incident.

2) <u>REGRET</u> — But he's <u>upset</u> and <u>regretful</u> when he remembers how <u>stupid</u> he felt after his dad's comments about the earring.

3) <u>AGREEMENT</u> — At the end of the poem, he seems to have come round to his <u>dad's point of view</u> — he now says the same kind of things to kids that his dad said to him.

Think About Your Feelings and Attitudes to the Poem

1) Pick 2 words or phrases that <u>stand out to you</u>. If none stand out, just pick 2 <u>unusual words or phrases</u>.

2) Write these 2 words or phrases down. Then write about how they <u>make you feel</u>. If they don't make you feel anything, don't worry — just <u>make something up</u>, as long as it's not too stupid.

> EXAMPLE When the poet says "It took a jeweller's gun / to pierce the flesh", it makes me wince with pain. It sounds like a horrible and pointless thing to put yourself through, just to try and look cool.

Themes — parent/child relationships, getting older, memory

Compare 'My father thought it...' with other poems about the same themes: <u>parent/child relationships</u> ('Before You Were Mine' p.44-45 and 'On my first Sonne' p.6-7), <u>getting older</u> ('Kid' p.60-61 and 'Mother, any distance...' p.52-53) and <u>memory</u> ('We Remember Your Childhood Well' p.46-47).

Section Three — Simon Armitage

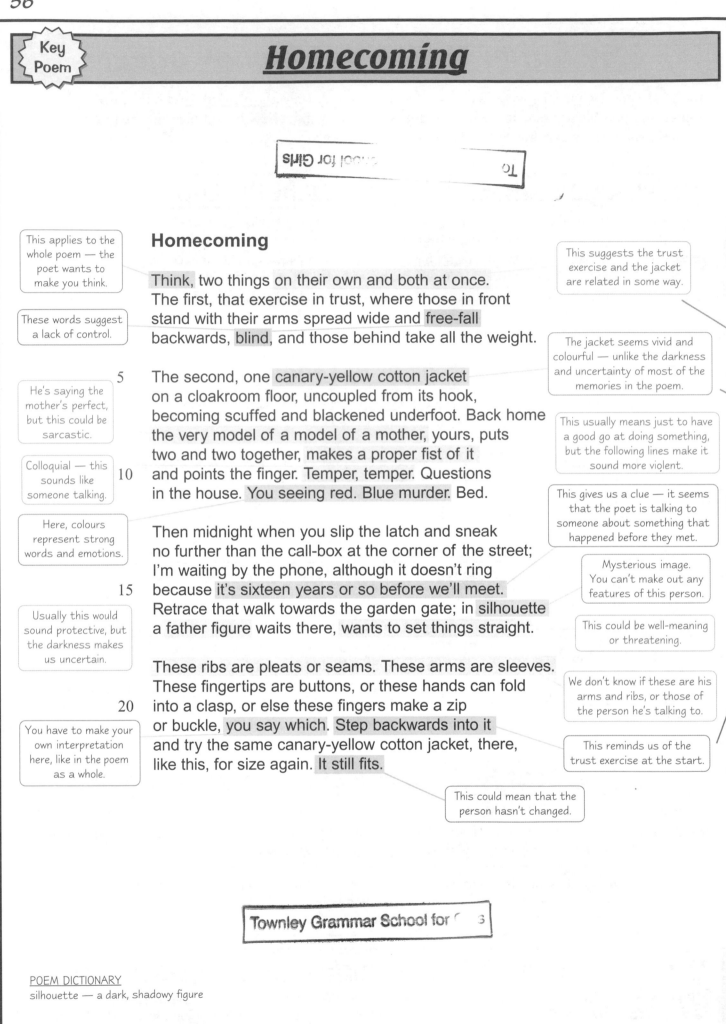

Key Poem

Homecoming

School for Girls   To

Homecoming

Think, two things on their own and both at once.
The first, that exercise in trust, where those in front
stand with their arms spread wide and free-fall
backwards, blind, and those behind take all the weight.

5 The second, one canary-yellow cotton jacket
on a cloakroom floor, uncoupled from its hook,
becoming scuffed and blackened underfoot. Back home
the very model of a model of a mother, yours, puts
two and two together, makes a proper fist of it
10 and points the finger. Temper, temper. Questions
in the house. You seeing red. Blue murder. Bed.

Then midnight when you slip the latch and sneak
no further than the call-box at the corner of the street;
I'm waiting by the phone, although it doesn't ring
15 because it's sixteen years or so before we'll meet.
Retrace that walk towards the garden gate; in silhouette
a father figure waits there, wants to set things straight.

These ribs are pleats or seams. These arms are sleeves.
These fingertips are buttons, or these hands can fold
20 into a clasp, or else these fingers make a zip
or buckle, you say which. Step backwards into it
and try the same canary-yellow cotton jacket, there,
like this, for size again. It still fits.

Annotations (left margin):

This applies to the whole poem — the poet wants to make you think.

These words suggest a lack of control.

He's saying the mother's perfect, but this could be sarcastic.

Colloquial — this sounds like someone talking.

Here, colours represent strong words and emotions.

Usually this would sound protective, but the darkness makes us uncertain.

You have to make your own interpretation here, like in the poem as a whole.

Annotations (right margin):

This suggests the trust exercise and the jacket are related in some way.

The jacket seems vivid and colourful — unlike the darkness and uncertainty of most of the memories in the poem.

This usually means just to have a good go at doing something, but the following lines make it sound more violent.

This gives us a clue — it seems that the poet is talking to someone about something that happened before they met.

Mysterious image. You can't make out any features of this person.

This could be well-meaning or threatening.

We don't know if these are his arms and ribs, or those of the person he's talking to.

This reminds us of the trust exercise at the start.

This could mean that the person hasn't changed.

Townley Grammar School for   3

POEM DICTIONARY
silhouette — a dark, shadowy figure

Homecoming

This is a pretty confusing poem because it's not very clear exactly what's happening. There are some hazy memories of people sneaking about and getting told off. A yellow jacket is described, which seems to be a metaphor for people changing over time.

You've Got to Know What Happens in the Poem

Lines 1-4   The poet describes an exercise where people learn to trust someone.

Lines 5-11   A yellow jacket lies on the floor somewhere getting trampled on. Then someone, probably a young woman, gets told off by their mum for doing something wrong.

Lines 12-17   The same person sneaks off again, this time to a phone box. A dark figure waits by a gate.

Lines 18-23   The different parts of the yellow jacket are described as if they're parts of someone's body. It seems that the person hasn't changed much, because the jacket still fits.

Learn About the Three Types of Language

1) **AMBIGUOUS LANGUAGE** — Lots of the images and description in the poem are ambiguous — we're not sure what they mean. This is often deliberate — it's supposed to make us stop and think about what the poet means.

2) **COLOUR** — Most of the images in the poem are dark and shadowy, reinforcing the vague and uncertain nature of the poem. The bright yellow colour of the jacket stands out.

3) **METAPHORICAL LANGUAGE** — The yellow jacket becomes a metaphor, possibly for behaviour or personality. The jacket still fits, so maybe the person the poet is talking to hasn't changed much.

Remember the Feelings and Attitudes in the Poem

"Err, hello, police? I'm being stalked by a poet..."

1) **ANGER** — The mother (lines 8-10) is very angry with her child.

2) **TENSION** — We don't know how the "father figure" is going to "set things straight" (line 17).

3) **UNCERTAINTY** — The poet wants us to make our own minds up about what the jacket stands for. We have to make the connections between the different things he describes.

Don't worry if you find this poem really confusing. You don't have to completely understand it — as long as you can make some interesting points about it.

Think About Your Feelings and Attitudes to the Poem

1) Pick 2 words or phrases that stand out to you. If none stand out, just pick 2 unusual words or phrases.

2) Write these 2 words or phrases down. Then write about how they make you feel. If they don't make you feel anything, don't worry — just make something up, as long as it's not too stupid.

EXAMPLE The line "a father figure waits there, wants to set things straight", makes me worry about the safety of the person in the poem. The way this person has to sneak around suggests he or she is afraid of someone, making the father figure's intentions sound menacing and dangerous.

Themes — memory, imagery and mood...

Compare 'Homecoming' with other poems about the same themes: memory ('Before You Were Mine' p.44-45 and 'We Remember Your Childhood Well' p.46-47), imagery ('Havisham' p.36-37 and 'Tichborne's Elegy' p.14-15) and mood ('Elvis's Twin Sister' p.38-39).

November

The year moves to its end, like the old people's lives.

Hints at the distress that the poet and John are feeling.

November

We walk to the ward from the badly parked car
with your grandma taking four short steps to our two.
We have brought her here to die and we know it.

Blunt statement that they can't ignore the sad truth of what's happening.

Uneven rhythm echoes her tiny steps.

They're "wrapping up" her life.

Double meaning — "it's the right time", and also "time has done this to these people".

5
You check her towel, soap and family trinkets,
pare her nails, parcel her in the rough blankets
and she sinks down into her incontinence.

Strong image of her physical helplessness.

Their whole bodies have stopped working properly.

It is time John. In their pasty bloodless smiles,
in their slack breasts, their stunned brains and their baldness,
and in us John: we are almost these monsters.

They will end up like this too. The matter-of-fact tone contrasts with the shocking word "monsters".

John's physically and emotionally broken by the experience.

10
You're shattered. You give me the keys and I drive
through the twilight zone, past the famous station
to your house, to numb ourselves with alcohol.

The darkness and run-down buildings surround them.

The fading light represents the knowledge that they too are getting older.

Inside and outside their minds, as well as the normal meanings.

Inside, we feel the terror of the dusk begin.
15
Outside we watch the evening, failing again,
and we let it happen. We can say nothing.

They're helpless to stop the ageing process and death.

There's only a brief flicker of light.

Sometimes the sun spangles and we feel alive.
One thing we have to get, John, out of this life.

Tries to take something positive out of the day's events.

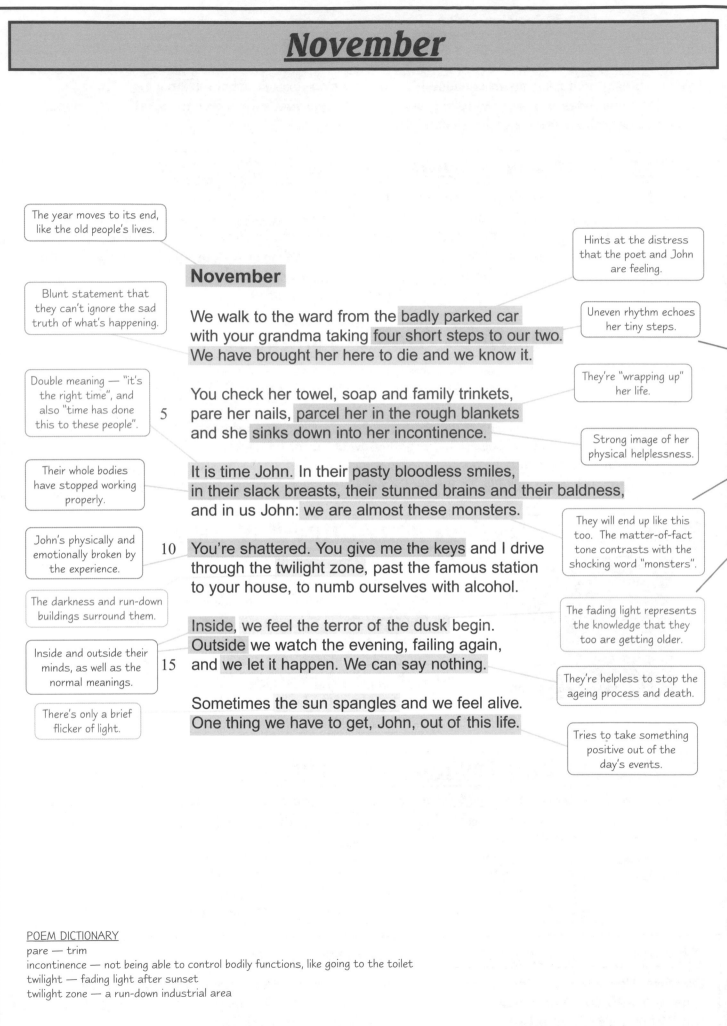

POEM DICTIONARY
pare — trim
incontinence — not being able to control bodily functions, like going to the toilet
twilight — fading light after sunset
twilight zone — a run-down industrial area

November

The poet writes about taking the grandmother of a person called John to live in a <u>nursing home</u>. The poet and John both know she won't be coming out again. The poet writes as if he's talking to John, and describes their sad thoughts on the journey back.

You've Got to Know What Happens in the Poem

<u>Lines 1-6</u>   The poet and John help John's grandma settle in at the home. She seems <u>weak</u> and <u>helpless</u>.

<u>Lines 7-9</u>   Other <u>old people</u> in the home are described. They are pale and seemingly <u>lifeless</u>.

<u>Lines 10-15</u> The poet and John go home. They feel really <u>depressed</u>, watching the night draw in.

<u>Lines 16-17</u> The poet says that we should <u>make the most</u> of the chances we get to <u>live</u>.

Learn About the Three Types of Language

1) <u>DECAY</u> — There are lots of images of things <u>breaking down</u>, e.g. the <u>health</u> of the old people. The title of the poem suggests the approaching cold weather, and reinforces the idea that the old people are in the <u>autumn years</u> of their lives.

2) <u>INEVITABILITY</u> — The poem is written in the <u>present tense</u>, as if it's happening now. This emphasises that growing old and dying is <u>inescapable</u> and <u>inevitable</u> — it's bound to happen eventually.

3) <u>DARKNESS</u> — The daylight fades away during the poem, suggesting the gradual approach of <u>death</u>. The gloomy setting also represents the poet's and John's <u>depressed thoughts</u>.

Remember the Feelings and Attitudes in the Poem

i) <u>HORROR</u> — The poet is <u>horrified</u> by the state of the old people.

2) <u>FEAR</u> — He's <u>depressed</u> and <u>frightened</u> by the thought of the same thing happening to him and everyone else (line 13).

3) <u>HELPLESSNESS</u> — He feels <u>helpless</u> to prevent an equally horrible end to his own life (line 15).

> The poet and John are <u>emotionally exhausted</u> at the end of the poem — they have to "numb" their pain with drink.

Think About Your Feelings and Attitudes to the Poem

1) Pick 2 words or phrases that <u>stand out to you</u>. If none stand out, just pick 2 <u>unusual words or phrases</u>.

2) Write these 2 words or phrases down. Then write about how they <u>make you feel</u>. If they don't make you feel anything, don't worry — just <u>make something up</u>, as long as it's not too stupid.

> **EXAMPLE**   I find the poet's comment, "we are almost these monsters", very shocking. Describing old people as "monsters" makes them sound totally inhuman and disgusting. Also the fact that he is "almost" like them suggests the poet will inevitably end up the same way.

Themes — death, attitudes to others, strong emotions...

Compare 'November' to other poems on the same themes: <u>death</u> ('Tichborne's Elegy' p.14-15 and 'Ulysses' p.26-27), <u>attitudes towards other people</u> ('Salome' p.42-43 and 'The Man He Killed' p.16-17) and <u>strong emotions</u> ('Havisham' p.36-37 and 'On my first Sonne' p.6-7).

Key Poem

Kid

Title suggests Batman and Robin could stand for a father and his son.

Alliteration emphasises sarcasm and contempt.

His tone is bitter when he describes how he was deserted.

The cliché of "letting the cat out of the bag" is changed slightly.

Combines the phrases "playing ball" and "ball boy" to stress how he used to do whatever Batman wanted.

Rhyme and rhythm make these words reflect his new strength and energy.

Imagines Batman eating basic, disgusting food on his own.

Robin enjoys patronising Batman.

Kid

Batman, big shot, when you gave the order
to grow up, then let me loose to wander
leeward, freely through the wild blue yonder
as you liked to say, or ditched me, rather,
5   in the gutter ... well, I turned the corner.
Now I've scotched that 'he was like a father
to me' rumour, sacked it, blown the cover
on that 'he was like an elder brother'
story, let the cat out on that caper
10   with the married woman, how you took her
downtown on expenses in the motor.
Holy robin-redbreast-nest-egg-shocker!
Holy roll-me-over-in-the-clover,
I'm not playing ball boy any longer
15   Batman, now I've doffed that off-the-shoulder
Sherwood-Forest-green and scarlet number
for a pair of jeans and crew-neck jumper;
now I'm taller, harder, stronger, older.
Batman, it makes a marvellous picture:
20   you without a shadow, stewing over
chicken giblets in the pressure cooker,
next to nothing in the walk-in larder,
punching the palm of your hand all winter,
you baby, now I'm the real boy wonder.

Batman claimed he was giving Robin his freedom.

Robin felt scared and alone.

First sign that he's beginning to take control.

Batman was supposed to catch criminals, but these phrases make it sound like he's the criminal.

These lines combine Robin's "holy" catchphrase with tabloid-headline style scandals.

Normal clothes show he's grown up and he's living in the real world now.

Robin was always inferior — but without him, Batman's alone.

Gloats about Batman's loneliness and frustration.

Robin was always called the "boy wonder", but now it has new meaning — Robin's in charge now.

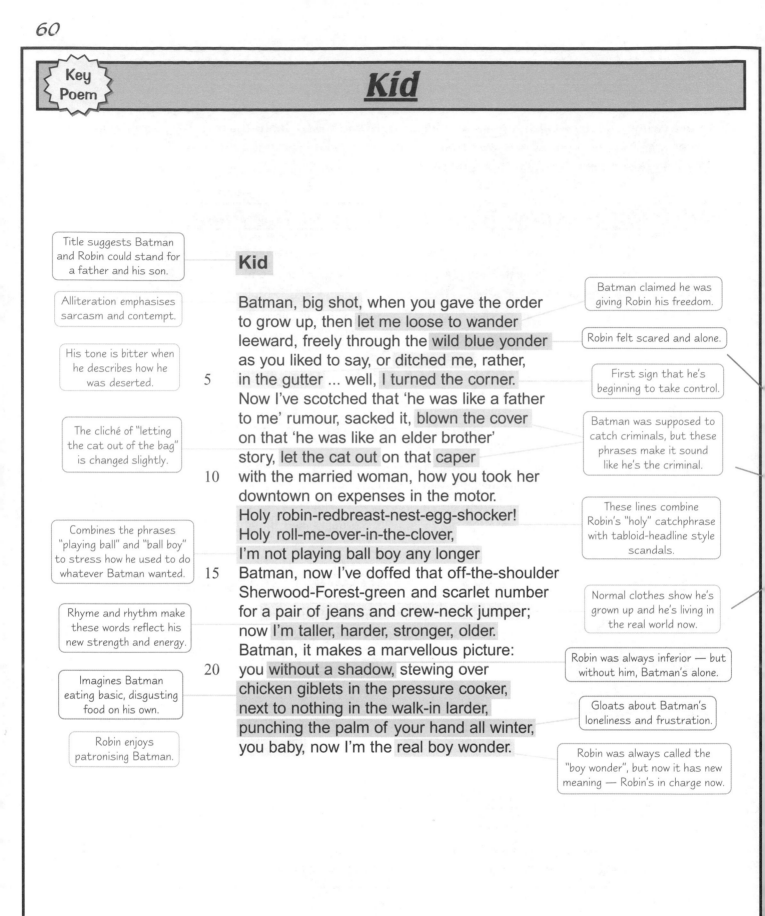

POEM DICTIONARY
leeward — towards the wind
scotched — put an end to
caper — a crime in a comic or film
on expenses — paid for by work
doffed — got rid of
giblets — the guts and insides of a chicken

Kid

This poem uses the superhero <u>Batman</u> and his sidekick <u>Robin</u> to stand for a young person who's been deserted by the person who was supposed to look after him. Now "Robin" is taking revenge, by showing that "Batman" wasn't such a hero after all. Holy poetry anthology!

You've Got to Know What Happens in the Poem

<u>Lines 1-5</u>	Robin (the narrator) is angry that Batman left him to <u>fend for himself</u> when he wasn't ready. But now Robin's <u>taking control</u> of his life.
<u>Lines 6-13</u>	Robin takes pleasure in revealing what Batman was <u>really like</u>. He <u>wasn't</u> a father figure to Robin as people had thought — he was taking out a <u>married woman</u> and claiming the money back from work.
<u>Lines 14-18</u>	Robin says he's not going to be Batman's <u>sidekick</u> any more. He's <u>grown up</u>, got rid of his silly costume and got some proper clothes.
<u>Lines 19-24</u>	Robin imagines Batman falling on hard times, and <u>gloats</u> when he pictures him <u>struggling</u>.

Learn About the Three Types of Language

1) <u>LANGUAGE ABOUT LONELINESS</u> — At first Robin describes <u>his own loneliness</u>, but by the end of the poem it's <u>Batman</u> who's <u>on his own</u>, in Robin's imagination at least.

2) <u>CLICHÉS</u> — There are a lot of commonly-used phrases and <u>clichés</u>, but they often <u>merge</u> together or end in an <u>unexpected</u> way. A lot of these phrases come from the <u>Batman</u> comics.

3) <u>BITTERNESS</u> and <u>SARCASM</u> — Robin's <u>bitter</u> and <u>annoyed</u> that everyone thinks Batman was so <u>great</u>. This is what makes him determined to get <u>revenge</u> by revealing the truth about him.

Remember the Feelings and Attitudes in the Poem

"I'm a bat, man."

1) <u>ANGER</u> — Robin is <u>angry</u> and <u>bitter</u> that Batman deserted him.

2) <u>DEFIANCE</u> — But he feels more <u>confident</u> now — he's <u>defiant</u> when he says he's "turned the corner".

3) <u>PRIDE</u> — Robin's <u>proud</u> of his new-found <u>independence</u>.

4) <u>PLEASURE</u> — He <u>enjoys</u> dishing the dirt on Batman, and <u>takes pleasure</u> from the idea of Batman being sad and alone.

Think About Your Feelings and Attitudes to the Poem

1) Pick 2 words or phrases that <u>stand out to you</u>. If none stand out, just pick 2 <u>unusual words or phrases</u>.

2) Write these 2 words or phrases down. Then write about how they <u>make you feel</u>. If they don't make you feel anything, don't worry — just <u>make something up</u>, as long as it's not too stupid.

> EXAMPLE When the Robin character says "I'm not playing ball boy any longer", I admire his determination. He feels very badly treated by "Batman", but instead of wallowing in self-pity, he has done something about it. I think that shows a lot of courage and self-belief.

Themes — getting older, memory and characters...

Compare 'Kid' with other poems about the same themes: <u>getting older</u> ('My father thought it...' p.54-55 and 'Mother, any distance...' p.52-53), <u>memory</u> ('Before You Were Mine' p.44-45 and 'My Last Duchess' p.22-23) and <u>characters</u> ('The Village Schoolmaster' p.28-29).

Those bastards in their mansions

from **Book of Matches**

Those bastards in their mansions:
to hear them shriek, you'd think
I'd poisoned the dogs and vaulted the ditches,
crossed the lawns in stocking feet and threadbare britches,
5   forced the door of one of the porches, and lifted
the gift of fire from the burning torches,

then given heat and light to streets and houses,
told the people how to ditch their cuffs and shackles,
armed them with the iron from their wrists and ankles.

10   Those lords and ladies in their palaces and castles,
they'd have me sniffed out by their beagles,
picked at by their eagles, pinned down, grilled
beneath the sun.

Me, I stick to the shadows, carry a gun.

Annotations (left side):

- He's totally open about his hatred for rich people.
- Makes them sound whingeing and pathetic.
- They think he's sneaky.
- He imagines breaking into their homes.
- He sees revolution as dramatic and heroic — he seems to think it's a pretty good idea.
- The upper class seem very distant and different to him.
- They want to contain and suppress him, to avoid a revolution.
- This sounds sinister, like he's waiting for his opportunity.

Annotations (right side):

- Suggests wealth and privilege, and this is what he really seems to hate.
- Double meaning — "vault" means jump over, but it also suggests the rich people's money.
- Another stereotype of rich houses. He suggests the ditches are there to keep him out.
- Stereotype of poverty.
- Suggests ordinary people are imprisoned by the rich.
- Stereotype that the upper class all hunt animals. He says they want to hunt him down in the same way.
- His intentions are far more brutal and less subtle than they imagined.

> This poem has references to the story of Prometheus. In Greek mythology, Prometheus stole fire from the gods to give to mankind. As a punishment, he was chained to a rock where an eagle tore at his liver.

POEM DICTIONARY
britches — trousers worn to the knee or just below
beagles — a breed of dog used for hunting

Section Three — Simon Armitage

Those bastards in their mansions

The person in this poem has really got it in for <u>rich people</u>. He says they treat him like he's trying to start a <u>revolution</u>. Turns out he's just lurking in the shadows. With a gun. So that's all right then.

You've Got to Know What Happens in the Poem

<u>Lines 1-6</u>   The person in the poem has a go at <u>rich people</u>. He says they treat him like he's a <u>criminal</u>.

<u>Lines 7-9</u>   He <u>denies</u> causing poor people to <u>revolt</u> — though it sounds like he'd like to.

<u>Lines 10-13</u>   He says that the rich want to <u>hunt him down</u> and imprison him.

<u>Line 14</u>   Rather than doing any of the things he's suspected of, he's <u>waiting for his chance</u> to strike.

Learn About the Three Types of Language

1) <u>STEREOTYPES</u> — His descriptions of rich and poor people are <u>simplified</u> and <u>exaggerated</u> — he sees the rich as living in big mansions, and imagines they in turn have a stereotyped image of the poor. He uses these <u>stereotypes</u> to emphasise how <u>different</u> they are to ordinary, working class people.

2) <u>REVOLUTIONARY LANGUAGE</u> — He sees ordinary, poor people as being <u>oppressed by the rich</u>. He says he <u>hasn't</u> been trying to start a <u>revolution</u>, i.e. getting the poor to take <u>power</u> from the rich. But the way he describes revolution suggests he actually thinks it would be a <u>good thing</u>.

3) <u>AGGRESSIVE LANGUAGE</u> — He has a lot of <u>violent</u>, <u>aggressive feelings</u> towards rich people. He describes the violent things he's been accused of, but <u>denies</u> they're true — until the last line.

Remember the Feelings and Attitudes in the Poem

"Go stop revolution, Rover."

1) <u>RESENTMENT</u> — The person in the poem <u>hates rich people</u>.

2) <u>OPPRESSION</u> — He says the rich <u>oppress ordinary people</u> — they control them with force.

3) <u>INDIGNATION</u> — He's <u>angry</u> about the things he's been <u>wrongly accused</u> of.

4) <u>REVENGE</u> — He wants to have his <u>revenge</u> on rich people.

Think About Your Feelings and Attitudes to the Poem

1) Pick 2 words or phrases that <u>stand out to you</u>. If none stand out, just pick 2 <u>unusual words or phrases</u>.

2) Write these 2 words or phrases down. Then write about how they <u>make you feel</u>. If they don't make you feel anything, don't worry — just <u>make something up</u>, as long as it's not too stupid.

> **EXAMPLE** When the person in the poem says "I stick to the shadows, carry a gun", it makes me feel both worried and excited. Having a gun shows he's plotting something very violent, which I find disturbing. But the way he waits in the shadows means we don't know when or how he will do it.

Themes — danger, attitudes to others and strong emotions

Compare 'Those bastards in their mansions' with other poems on the same themes: <u>danger</u> ('Education for Leisure' p.48-49 and 'Stealing' p.50-51), <u>attitudes towards other people</u> ('Hitcher' p.66-67) and <u>strong emotions</u> ('The Song of the Old Mother' p.8-9).

Section Three — Simon Armitage

64

I've made out a will

from **Book of Matches**

We expect him to say he's leaving valuable items, but instead he leaves his body.

Humorously says his insides must be useful.

Rhyming adds to the light-hearted tone.

The exact amount reminds us of the will theme.

Could mean ribcage, or that people are trapped by their bodies' limitations.

I've made out a will; I'm leaving myself
to the National Health. I'm sure they can use
the jellies and tubes and syrups and glues,
the web of nerves and veins, the loaf of brains,
5   and assortment of fillings and stitches and wounds,
blood – a gallon exactly of bilberry soup –
the chassis or cage or cathedral of bone;
but not the heart, they can leave that alone.

Cockney rhyming slang — loaf of bread = head.

His body is far from perfect.

Light-heartedly describes the deep colour of blood.

Reminds us of the saying "Your body is a temple" — you should look after it.

Blunt tone makes his feelings clear.

Sounds like his body's a shop, and the parts are goods.

Here the poet describes his body like it's a car engine, with lots of complicated parts.

Returns to the theme of a will, but leaves the heart where it is instead of leaving it to someone.

They can have the lot, the whole stock:
10 the loops and coils and sprockets and springs and rods,
the twines and cords and strands,
the face, the case, the cogs and the hands,

but not the pendulum, the ticker;
leave that where it stops or hangs.

The body is just clothing — it's not important.

The body is described like a clock.

Reminds us of the heart's regular beat, and also that life is ticking away.

The poem ends on the serious subject of death.

POEM DICTIONARY
bilberry — a dark blue fruit
chassis — the frame of a car
sprockets — wheels on a chain

Section Three — Simon Armitage

I've made out a will

The poet has written a <u>will</u> — but instead of saying who he's leaving his possessions to, he says he's leaving his <u>body</u> to the NHS. It's quite humorous, but has a serious point — he says the NHS can have everything but his heart, which is the only part of his body that's important to him.

You've Got to Know What Happens in the Poem

<u>Lines 1-8</u> The poet describes all the different things in his <u>body</u>, in a disgusting but comical way. He says the National Health Service can have <u>everything</u> apart from his <u>heart</u>.

<u>Lines 9-12</u> He compares his body to an <u>engine</u> (line 10), <u>clothes</u> (line 11) and a <u>clock</u> (line 12).

<u>Lines 13-14</u> The poem ends on a more <u>serious</u> note, by reminding us of the suddenness of <u>death</u>.

Learn About the Three Types of Language

1) <u>LANGUAGE RELATED TO WILLS</u> — There are a few little <u>phrases</u> thrown in which give the poem the feel of a <u>will</u>. This reinforces the theme of the poem.

2) <u>HUMOROUS LANGUAGE</u> — There are quite a lot of <u>funny descriptions</u>, even though they're often about pretty <u>disgusting</u> things like blood and guts. This allows the poet to talk about death, which could be a pretty depressing subject, in a <u>light-hearted</u> way.

3) <u>METAPHORICAL LANGUAGE</u> — The body is described as if it's various different things, such as an <u>engine</u>, a <u>clock</u> and a <u>cathedral</u>. This helps the poet give a certain <u>impression</u> of the body and its different parts.

Remember the Feelings and Attitudes in the Poem

Anyone for jelly?

1) <u>HUMOUR</u> — The poet has a <u>light-hearted</u> attitude towards his body.
2) <u>FEARLESSNESS</u> — He's <u>not bothered</u> about the prospect of <u>death</u>.
3) <u>SENTIMENTALITY</u> — He has an emotional <u>attachment</u> to his <u>heart</u>.

> The poet's feelings about his heart could refer to its connection to love — although he doesn't say this outright.

Think About Your Feelings and Attitudes to the Poem

1) Pick 2 words or phrases that <u>stand out to you</u>. If none stand out, just pick 2 <u>unusual words or phrases</u>.

2) Write these 2 words or phrases down. Then write about how they <u>make you feel</u>. If they don't make you feel anything, don't worry — just <u>make something up</u>, as long as it's not too stupid.

> **EXAMPLE** I find the poet's description of "the jellies and tubes and syrups and glues" in his body sickening. It's a very unpleasant way of describing what people's bodies are made of.

Themes — death, imagery and the first person...

Compare 'I've made out a will' with other poems about the same themes: <u>death</u> ('November' p.58-59 and 'Tichborne's Elegy' p.14-15), <u>imagery</u> ('Havisham' p.36-37 and 'Sonnet 130' p.20-21) and use of the <u>first person</u> ('Education for Leisure' p.48-49 and 'Homecoming' p.56-57).

Hitcher

Key Poem

Hitcher

The narrator is trying to get away from stress at work.

The narrator's problems come to him via modern technology — the hitcher lives a simpler life.

I'd been tired, under
the weather, but the ansaphone kept screaming:
One more sick-note, mister, and you're finished. Fired.
I thumbed a lift to where the car was parked.
5 A Vauxhall Astra. It was hired.

Before he kills the hitcher, the killer himself hitches a lift.

Rhyming words emphasise pressure from work.

I picked him up in Leeds.
He was following the sun to west from east
with just a toothbrush and the good earth for a bed. The truth,
he said, was blowin' in the wind,
10 or round the next bend.

Romantic image of travelling.

The hitcher is relaxed and dreamy, unlike the narrator.

I let him have it
on the top road out of Harrogate – once
with the head, then six times with the krooklok
in the face – and didn't even swerve.
15 I dropped it into third

The violence is shocking because it comes suddenly — there's no build-up to it.

He hits the hitcher repeatedly — it's a savage, sustained attack.

Sounds like he's boasting.

and leant across
to let him out, and saw him in the mirror
bouncing off the kerb, then disappearing down the verge.
We were the same age, give or take a week.
20 He'd said he liked the breeze

Pretends he's being considerate.

Disturbing image, but his matter-of-fact tone suggests he's not bothered by it.

Another connection between him and the hitcher, but it doesn't matter to him.

to run its fingers
through his hair. It was twelve noon.
The outlook for the day was moderate to fair.
Stitch that, I remember thinking,
25 you can walk from there.

Makes fun of the hitcher's dreamy attitude.

Could be a play on words — the hitcher will need a few stitches if he's still alive.

The rhyming here shows the narrator is more relaxed than at the start of the poem.

POEM DICTIONARY
Krooklok — metal device used to prevent car theft

Hitcher

Key Poem

The chap in this poem isn't an awfully nice fella. He picks up a <u>hitch-hiker</u> — ok so far — then duffs him up, chucks him out of his car while it's still going and <u>leaves him for dead</u>. And the moral of the story is: if you're in Leeds, get the bus.

You've Got to Know What Happens in the Poem

<u>Lines 1-5</u>	The narrator was feeling <u>under pressure</u> as he hitched a lift to the car he'd hired.
<u>Lines 6-10</u>	He describes picking a <u>hitch-hiker</u> up, and the <u>easy-going</u> lifestyle the hitcher was leading.
<u>Lines 11-18</u>	He tells us he <u>beat up</u> the hitcher while he was still driving, then <u>pushed him out</u> of the car.
<u>Lines 19-25</u>	He jokes that the <u>weather's nice</u> so the hitcher can <u>walk</u> the rest of the way.

Learn About the Four Types of Language

1) <u>CONTRASTS</u> — The simple, <u>relaxed</u> life of the hitcher contrasts with the <u>stress</u> the narrator feels.

2) <u>VIOLENT LANGUAGE</u> — The narrator describes quite <u>graphically</u> how he <u>attacked</u> the hitcher. His descriptions are particularly shocking because of the <u>casual tone</u> of voice he uses.

3) <u>FLIPPANT REMARKS</u> — He makes some pretty <u>flippant comments</u> and <u>sick jokes</u> about the assault. He <u>makes fun</u> of the hitcher for his easy-going <u>lifestyle</u>.

4) <u>LINKS</u> — There are some <u>similarities</u> between the narrator and the hitcher.

Remember the Feelings and Attitudes in the Poem

One more sick note Mr...

1) <u>STRESS</u> — At the start of the poem, the narrator feels irritable, ill and <u>under pressure</u>.

2) <u>DETACHMENT</u> — His matter-of-fact tone shows he <u>doesn't feel bad</u> about what he does.

3) <u>JEALOUSY</u> — He <u>envies</u> the hitch-hiker's relaxed lifestyle and hates him for it.

4) <u>SPITE</u> — His nasty joke at the end suggests he takes a <u>sick pleasure</u> from killing the hitch-hiker.

Think About Your Feelings and Attitudes to the Poem

1) Pick 2 words or phrases that <u>stand out to you</u>. If none stand out, just pick 2 <u>unusual words or phrases</u>.

2) Write these 2 words or phrases down. Then write about how they <u>make you feel</u>. If they don't make you feel anything, don't worry — just <u>make something up</u>, as long as it's not too stupid.

> **EXAMPLE** When the narrator describes the hitcher "bouncing off the kerb, then disappearing down the verge", I feel shocked. This is a horrible image. Even though he knows he has probably killed the hitcher, the narrator describes it as if it is a perfectly normal sight.

Themes — mood, evil and attitudes towards other people...

Compare 'Hitcher' with other poems about the same themes: <u>mood</u> ('Havisham' p.36-37 and 'Education for Leisure' p.48-49), <u>evil</u> ('My Last Duchess' p.22-23 and 'The Laboratory' p.30-31) and <u>attitudes towards other people</u> ('The Song of the Old Mother' p.8-9 and 'Stealing' p.50-51).

Section Three — Simon Armitage

Death

Death is something people feel <u>emotional</u> about — so it's a good theme for poetry.

> 1) The death of a loved one causes <u>grief</u> and a sense of <u>loss</u>.
> 2) Everyone dies — it's something we need to <u>prepare</u> for.
> 3) Deaths caused by <u>war, crime or execution</u> can seem an unnecessary waste of life.

Some Poets write about Killing and Murder

Education for Leisure (Pages 48-49)

1) The poet writes from the point of view of a <u>psychopath</u> who's planning to "kill something".
2) The character usually has a <u>dull life</u> — feeling "ignored" and suffering from "boredom".
3) The character gets <u>obsessed</u> with the <u>power of killing</u>. It makes their life feel more <u>exciting</u>. They imagine themselves as a "genius" and a "superstar".
4) At the end of the poem, the character seems to <u>threaten the reader</u>: "I touch your arm."

The Man He Killed (Pages 16-17)

1) In this poem, a soldier talks about a man he <u>killed during a battle</u>. He points out the <u>irony</u> that if he had met the man in other circumstances, they might have been friends.
2) He imagines that the man he killed was rather <u>like himself</u>. He might have only enlisted in the army because he was unemployed and needed a job. Even though officially the man was his "foe", there wasn't necessarily anything bad about him.
3) The poem points out how <u>foolish and wasteful</u> the <u>killing in war</u> is: "You shoot a fellow down / You'd treat if met where any bar is".

Maybe we should just go for a pint.

Death can be Depressing

On my first Sonne (Pages 6-7)

1) The poet expresses the <u>grief</u> he feels over the <u>loss of a child</u>: "Farewell, thou child of my right hand, and joy".
2) The poet tries to find something <u>positive</u> in his son's death — that at least the boy has escaped many of life's troubles and old age.
3) He pays <u>tribute</u> to his son by saying he was "his best piece of poetrie" — his best work. He vows never to love anything so much again, in case he loses it.

November (Pages 58-59)

1) Seeing the <u>old people</u> in the home makes the poet think about his <u>own death</u>.
2) The old people appear to be very <u>close to death</u> — their "pasty bloodless smiles" and "stunned brains" suggest that some parts of their bodies are <u>already</u> dead.
3) The thought of death <u>depresses</u> the poet — "we feel the terror of the dusk begin."
4) But at the end he says, "sometimes the sun spangles", and this makes him <u>determined</u> to get as much out of life as possible <u>before he dies</u>.

This topic's a bit bleak...

Other poems which talk about death are: 'Tichborne's Elegy' (p.14-15), 'The Laboratory' (p.30-31), 'Salome' (p.42-43) and 'Hitcher' (p.66-67). They fall into two camps — 1) poets feeling awful about people dying in real life, and 2) poets writing from the point of view of a crazed killer.

Parent/Child Relationships

Family arguments — a great source of poetic inspiration.

1) The parent/child relationship is <u>central</u> to most people's lives.
2) Parent/child relationships often <u>change</u> as people grow older.
3) Some children struggle for <u>independence</u> from their parents.

Parents Find it Hard to Let Go

Mother, any distance (Pages 52-53)

1) The person in this poem is moving into his <u>own house</u>. He's becoming <u>independent</u> from his mum.
2) His mum helps him <u>measure</u> things. The tape measure, "unreeling / years between us", becomes a metaphor for all their <u>shared memories</u> and history.
3) His mother finds it <u>difficult to let go</u> of him completely: "your fingertips still pinch / the last one-hundredth of an inch".
4) At the end, he faces up to <u>life without his mum</u>. He's ready "to fall or fly".

The Affliction of Margaret (Pages 10-11)

1) The woman in the poem hasn't heard from her son for <u>7 years</u>.
2) We see the mother's <u>anguish</u> at not knowing whether her son is <u>dead or alive</u>.
3) She's <u>desperate</u> to hear from him, whatever has happened to him: "Oh find me, prosperous or undone!"
4) She describes her son as if he's almost <u>perfect</u>: "He was among the prime in worth."
5) She dearly <u>loves</u> her son, but we <u>don't</u> find out how he feels about her.

Children's Views of their Parents Change Over Time

My father thought it bloody queer (Pages 54-55)

1) The poet remembers his <u>father's anger</u> and <u>sarcasm</u> when he "rolled home with a ring of silver" in his ear. He was hurt and upset by his father's reaction.
2) When the earring became <u>sore and painful</u>, he started to realise his father might have been right.
3) Now the poet's older, he finds himself <u>giving the same advice</u> as his father did: *"If I were you, / I'd take it out and leave it out next year."*

Parents make Sacrifices for their Children

Tidy your room, luv.

Before You Were Mine (Pages 44-45)

1) The poet imagines her <u>mother</u> as a <u>glamorous young woman</u> in the 1950s, looking and behaving like "Marilyn".
2) She likes to think of her mother as a bit of a <u>rebel</u> who <u>put pleasure first</u>. She imagines her staying out late, not caring that she would get "a hiding" when she came home.
3) She remembers as a child, playing with her mum's high-heeled shoes, "<u>relics</u>" of her frivolous past, and her mum teaching her to "*Cha cha cha*" on the way back from Church.
4) She realises the <u>sacrifices</u> her mother's made since her <u>birth</u>. With the "loud, possessive yell" of a <u>young baby</u>, she took over her mum's life. Her mum no longer had time to go out and have a good time.

Everyone starts off as a squalling baby...

Other poems which describe parent/child relationships are 'On my first Sonne' (p.6-7), 'We Remember Your Childhood Well' (p.46-47) and 'Kid' (p.60-61).

Danger

Some people are <u>scared</u> by danger — others get a <u>kick out of it</u>.

> 1) Danger can arise from the <u>natural environment</u>, e.g. storms, earthquakes and floods.
> 2) Danger can also be <u>caused by people</u> — through aggression and violence.
> 3) Some people find danger and risk-taking <u>exciting</u> (we don't endorse this attitude...).

People can Find Themselves in Dangerous Situations

The Little Boy Lost and The Little Boy Found (Pages 12-13)

1) The little boy is <u>helpless</u> on his own — "the mire was deep".
2) The danger is <u>averted</u> when <u>God</u> appears, "like his father in white".
3) Blake uses the story to make his <u>moral</u> clear — he says we're <u>lost without God</u>.

Patrolling Barnegat (Pages 18-19)

1) The poem describes a small band of watchmen patrolling the beach during a <u>fierce storm</u>.
2) The storm is described as very <u>powerful</u>: "Waves, air, midnight, their savagest trinity lashing". It is an <u>uncontrollable</u> part of nature: "Wild, wild the storm".
3) The storm is <u>dangerous</u> — out to sea the watchmen wonder if they can see a <u>wrecked ship</u>: "is that a wreck? is the red signal flaring?".

Some Poets write about Dangerous People

Hitcher (Pages 66-67)

1) The poem is written from the <u>point of view of a murderer</u> who kills a hitch-hiker.
2) At first, the murderer sounds like an <u>ordinary man</u>. He moans about everyday things: "I'd been tired, under / the weather".
3) Then as the story unfolds, it becomes clear that the murderer is a <u>dangerous criminal</u>. He's <u>planned the murder</u> in advance, hiring a car to do the murder in.
4) The hitch-hiker is <u>unaware of the danger</u> he's in. He talks happily to the murderer about his life and aspirations: "The truth, / he said, was blowin' in the wind".
5) The murder is <u>brutal and shocking</u>, especially because the murderer himself doesn't seem shocked by it: "I let him have it / on the top road out of Harrogate".

Danger and Risk-Taking can be Exciting

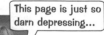

This page is just so darn depressing...

Stealing (Pages 50-51)

1) The poem is written from the point of view of a <u>young thief</u>.
2) There <u>isn't any point</u> to the thief's law-breaking: "I steal things I don't need. I joy-ride cars / to nowhere".
3) The only reason the thief does it is for the "<u>thrill</u>" — they describe the <u>excitement</u> they feel from standing in "A stranger's bedroom. Mirrors. I sigh like this — *Aah*."
4) When they're not stealing, the thief feels <u>bored</u>: "Mostly I'm so bored I could eat myself."

People do strange things for kicks...

This is a bit of a grim topic: people being frightened and getting hurt. If you want more of this doleful stuff, then have a look at these poems: 'The Laboratory' (p.30-31), 'Education for Leisure' (p.48-49) and 'Those bastards in their mansions' (p.62-63).

Attitudes Towards Other People

Poems are often about the poets' attitudes and feelings towards other people. Sometimes their attitude towards others is very positive and warm, other times it's very nasty indeed...

> 1) Some poets write about <u>positive</u> attitudes and feelings towards other people.
> 2) Some poets write about <u>negative or violent</u> attitudes towards other people.
> 3) Sometimes poets write about their attitudes towards other people <u>changing</u>.

Poems can be about Positive Attitudes towards Others

Anne Hathaway (Pages 40-41)

1) The poem is written from the <u>point of view of Shakespeare's wife</u>, remembering her <u>dead husband</u>.
2) Her <u>attitude</u> towards him is very <u>loving</u> and <u>affectionate</u>. She describes him as "my living laughing love", as if he is still alive. The word "laughing" emphasises how much she enjoyed his company.
3) She has <u>fond memories</u> of how he made her feel. She describes how spending time with him was like going to a magical land: "a spinning world / of forests, castles, torchlight".
4) Even now he's dead, she <u>won't forget him</u>: she carries the memories in "the casket of my widow's head".

Poems can portray Negative Attitudes towards Others

Those bastards in their mansions (Pages 62-63)

1) The character in the poem <u>hates</u> rich, upper class "bastards".
2) He has a <u>stereotyped</u> view of them — "Those lords and ladies in their palaces and castles".
3) He sees rich people as <u>bullies</u> who would "have me sniffed out by their beagles".
4) He also suggests that they're a bit <u>paranoid</u> and <u>pathetic</u>, as they "shriek" about him breaking into their houses.

Kid (Pages 60-61)

1) The Robin character <u>hates Batman</u> because he "ditched" him when Robin still needed him.
2) Robin thinks other people had a <u>false impression</u> of Batman. Robin says he's "scotched that 'he was like a father / to me' rumour" and shown everyone what Batman's <u>really like</u>.
3) Robin sees Batman as <u>selfish</u> and <u>irresponsible</u> for neglecting him. He also sees him as <u>immoral</u> — he was taking a married woman "downtown on expenses in the motor".
4) At the end of the poem, Robin portrays Batman as a <u>loser</u>, living on his own <u>eating rubbish</u>: "you without a shadow, stewing over / chicken giblets in the pressure cooker".

The Laboratory (Pages 30-31)

1) The woman in the poem feels <u>really angry</u> towards her <u>lover</u> and his <u>new mistress</u>. She thinks they've made a <u>fool</u> of her: "they laugh, laugh at me".
2) She's intent on <u>revenge</u> and wants to use poison to <u>kill</u> the mistress in a <u>painful way</u>: "Let death be felt and the proof remain". Through killing his mistress, she hopes to <u>hurt</u> her lover as well: "He is sure to remember her dying face!"
3) She is <u>excited</u> about the idea of killing and getting revenge. She feels <u>no guilt</u> about what she is doing.

"Mad, moi?"

Anger, resentment, love, lust, hate, jealousy, contempt...

Poems which show characters' attitudes towards other people include: 'Stealing' (p.50-51), 'Hitcher' (p.66-67) and 'The Song of the Old Mother' (p.8-9).

<u>Love</u>

There are a few poems on the good old-fashioned theme of love in this anthology, but <u>not</u> <u>many</u> of them are <u>romantic</u>. Some of them are about love between people in families, some of them describe love of nature, or even love of crime...

> 1) Some poets write about <u>romantic love</u>.
> 2) Poets also write about <u>family love</u>, e.g. between mother and son.
> 3) Some poets write about their love of <u>nature</u>, or a particular <u>place</u> or <u>pastime</u>.

Some Poems are about Romantic Love

Sonnet 130 (Pages 20-21)

1) This poem is a <u>sonnet</u> (it's 14 lines long). Sonnet form is often used for <u>love poetry</u>.
2) In the first part of the poem, Shakespeare <u>goes against the reader's expectations</u> of a love sonnet. He's <u>pretty rude</u> about his mistress, e.g. he says her "eyes are nothing like the sun", her hair is like "black wires" and her breath "reeks".
3) On line 9, he says "I love to hear her speak". This is the <u>first hint</u> that he <u>does love his mistress</u>.
4) In the last two lines, the tone changes. Shakespeare declares that his mistress is <u>just as wonderful</u> as <u>any woman</u> who's <u>praised</u> with <u>silly compliments</u>: "I think my love as rare / As any she belied with false compare."

Anne Hathaway (Pages 40-41)

1) This poem is a <u>sonnet</u>, a traditional form for a love poem.
2) Anne Hathaway describes the love between her and her <u>husband</u> Shakespeare, before he died.
3) The love between them was almost <u>too good to be true</u>. Anne uses <u>romantic</u>, <u>magical words</u> to describe it: "my lover's words / were shooting stars".
4) She says their love was "Romance / and drama played by touch, by scent, by taste" — their love was so <u>passionate</u> she felt as if they were characters in one of her husband's <u>plays</u>.

Some Poems are about Love of Places or Nature

Sonnet (Pages 34-35)

1) The poet describes how much he <u>loves the countryside</u> in <u>summer</u>.
2) He starts three lines with the phrase "<u>I love</u>" which emphasises his feelings.
3) He describes the countryside in a very <u>positive way</u>, using words like "beaming", "happy" and "bright" to show how much he likes it.

Inversnaid (Pages 32-33)

1) The poet describes a place with <u>wild, natural scenery</u>, with a "darksome burn" rolling through the hills.
2) In the final stanza, the poet makes an appeal for places like this to be left alone. He <u>loves</u> the "<u>wilderness</u>" and wants it to survive.

"Who cares about boys? I love shrubbery..."

<u>Some Poets love Wolverhampton Wanderers...</u>

The poems in this anthology are pretty bleak — there aren't many about love. Other poems you could look at are: 'On my first Sonne' (p.6-7), 'The Affliction of Margaret' (p.10-11), 'Mother, any distance' (p.52-53), and... no, that's it.

Memory

Many poems are based around memories — of <u>people</u>, <u>events</u> and <u>feelings</u>.

1) Memories can be associated with many <u>different feelings</u>, e.g. pride, shame, joy or anger.
2) People sometimes <u>block out bad memories</u>.
3) Memories can be <u>unreliable</u> — you might remember things differently to how they actually happened.

Memories can be Unreliable and Confusing

Homecoming (Pages 56-57)

1) This poem is deliberately <u>ambiguous</u>. It encourages the reader to "Think" in the first line, and then presents a <u>series of images</u>, many of which seem to be from the <u>past</u>. The clearest story is about a mother getting angry with her child — the child goes to bed angry and then sneaks off at night.
2) The poem <u>plays around with time</u>. The poet says he's there the night the person sneaks out, but there isn't any contact between them "because it's sixteen years or so before we'll meet."
3) The poet says the person should "<u>Retrace</u> that walk towards the garden gate". This suggests the <u>homecoming</u> of the poem's title. Maybe the child who sneaked away is returning home as an adult.
4) The end of the poem suggests that the person is going <u>back to their old life</u> and the character they used to be. An <u>old yellow jacket</u> seems to <u>symbolise</u> the person's <u>old life</u>. The poet encourages them to step back into it: "It still fits."

We Remember Your Childhood Well (Pages 46-47)

1) This poem is about someone telling someone else that his or her <u>memories</u> are <u>wrong</u>.
2) It seems likely that there is a <u>reason</u> why the memories are being denied — perhaps to cover up mistreatment or abuse that happened in the past.
3) The memories are only <u>hinted</u> at, which makes us think the <u>worst</u> about what happened, e.g. the phrase "Nobody forced you" sounds really sinister.

The Village Schoolmaster (Pages 28-29)

1) The poet points out the "<u>straggling fence</u>" next to where the school was. This makes him remember the <u>schoolmaster</u>.
2) The schoolmaster was "a man severe" — he <u>doesn't</u> sound particularly <u>friendly</u>. But he had bags of <u>knowledge</u> and a wide range of <u>skills</u>.
3) Memories of the schoolmaster are <u>unclear</u> in places, e.g. the poet says "the story ran that he could gauge", suggesting no-one was quite <u>sure</u> about him.
4) The schoolmaster seems <u>mysterious</u> — he "Amazed the gazing rustics".

Some Memories inspire Pride and Affection

Ulysses (Pages 26-27)

1) Ulysses has returned to his home of Ithaca after years spent away. He finds normal life <u>boring</u> and wants to return to travelling and adventure.
2) Ulysses has <u>strong memories</u> of the <u>glory</u> of his former life. He remembers the "drunk delight of battle" and all that he has "seen and known".
3) In the past, he became <u>famous</u> and had an <u>impact on events</u>. He says, "I am a part of all that I have met".
4) He's <u>proud</u> of his former achievements. Memories of his past glory inspire him to go travelling again: "I cannot rest from travel: I will drink / Life to the lees".

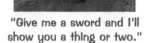
"Give me a sword and I'll show you a thing or two."

I remember it well...

"Memories, like the corners of my mind..." How does the rest of that song go? Ah well. Another poem which deals with memories is 'Before You Were Mine' (p.44-45). And don't forget it.

Evil

Evil is a good subject for poems because it's <u>dramatic</u> and <u>extreme</u>.

> 1) Some characters seem to kill just for <u>fun</u>.
> 2) Others become <u>obsessed</u> with <u>revenge</u>, and will do anything to get it.
> 3) Some characters appear quite <u>normal</u>, but give us little <u>glimpses</u> that they're not quite the ticket.

Some Characters are Openly Evil

The Laboratory (Pages 30-31)

1) The woman in this poem suspects her husband or lover has been <u>unfaithful</u> to her.
2) She's determined to get <u>revenge</u> by <u>poisoning</u> the other woman.
3) She's very <u>nasty</u> — she's prepared to <u>murder</u> the other woman just to <u>get her own back</u> on her lover. She sounds <u>pleased</u> when she says "He is sure to remember her dying face!"

Hitcher (Pages 66-67)

1) The killer <u>plans</u> the murder in advance — he's arranged a <u>hire car</u> for it.
2) His <u>attitude</u> to the killing is <u>shocking</u> — he sounds calm when he describes it, rather than angry or worked up. This suggests it might <u>not</u> be the <u>first time</u> he's done this.
3) The nature of the violence is <u>barbaric</u> — he headbutts him, then hits him "six times with the krooklok / in the face". He seems to <u>enjoy</u> watching the hitcher "bouncing off the kerb".
4) He callously <u>mocks</u> the hitcher's attitude after attacking him: "He'd said he liked the breeze / to run its fingers / through his hair." He seems to think that the hitcher's lifestyle is <u>reason enough</u> to attack him.

Some Characters Gradually Reveal their Evil Side

My Last Duchess (Pages 22-23)

1) The Duke is showing a guest a <u>portrait</u> of his <u>dead wife</u>. He seems <u>pleasant</u> and <u>polite</u>.
2) But we gradually realise there's something <u>fishy</u> about him. He starts to <u>criticise</u> the Duchess for the way she acted: "her looks went everywhere".
3) The Duke says the Duchess treated him <u>no better</u> than anyone else — he seems really <u>jealous</u>.
4) He sounds <u>sinister</u> when he tells his guest: "I gave commands; / Then all smiles stopped together." This makes it sound like he <u>murdered</u> his wife just because he didn't like her <u>flirting</u> with other men.

Salome (Pages 42-43)

Go on, chop his head off.

1) The woman in this poem has <u>cut off a man's head</u>.
2) She seems <u>mildly regretful</u> at first, but we think this is because she's <u>slept with a stranger</u>.
3) When it turns out she's actually <u>beheaded</u> the man, we see what she's said in a different context. She says she'd "done it before" and she'll "do it again" — she's a <u>serial murderer</u>.
4) She <u>can't remember</u> who the man is: "a head on the pillow beside me – whose? – / what did it matter?" This suggests that she kills <u>randomly</u>, rather than having anything in particular against her victims.

I call him "Mini-Simon-Armitage"...

Yep, this anthology's certainly got a dark side. Other poems about evil are: 'Havisham' (p.36-37) and 'Education for Leisure' (p.48-49). But remember — don't have nightmares.

Getting Older

This theme falls into two camps: poems about growing up, and poems about ageing.

> 1) <u>Growing up</u> and becoming <u>independent</u> from your parents can be a <u>difficult</u> time.
>
> 2) <u>Growing old</u> and realising you've not got much time left can be <u>depressing</u>.

Growing Up can be a Difficult Time

Mother, any distance (Pages 52-53)

1) The character in this poem is <u>moving into a new house</u> for the first time.
2) He asks his <u>mum</u> to help him <u>measure the new house</u>. His mum stands at the bottom of the stairs holding a tape measure as her son walks up the stairs, holding the other end.
3) This situation is used as a <u>metaphor</u> for the character <u>gaining independence</u> from his mum. The <u>tape measure</u> represents the <u>bond</u> between them. For a long time, his mother keeps hanging onto the end of the tape measure ("your fingertips still pinch / the last one-hundredth of an inch") — this represents the way she is <u>clinging on to her son</u>.
4) There comes a point when the character needs to <u>let go</u> of the tape measure, because it won't stretch any further. He realises that he has to <u>take risks for himself</u>: "to fall or fly" without his mum there to help him.

Kid (Pages 60-61)

1) The character in this poem feels that he was <u>let down</u> by the person who was supposed to look after him when he was young.
2) He says he was given "<u>the order / to grow up</u>" — expected to be independent before he was ready.
3) The character says he's now grown up and <u>made a success of himself</u>: "now I'm taller, harder, stronger, older." But he's <u>still</u> <u>bitter</u> about his experience of adolescence.

Growing Old Isn't Much Fun Either

Ulysses (Pages 26-27)

1) Ulysses has returned home as a <u>hero</u> after ten years <u>travelling back from the Trojan war</u>.
2) He's <u>bored</u> of being "an idle king" though, and wants to <u>continue his adventures</u> until he dies.
3) He knows he's <u>not as strong and fit</u> as he used to be, and he's aware that <u>death</u> isn't far away. But this <u>doesn't put him off</u> — he tells his crew that he is still "strong in will".
4) Ulysses <u>isn't</u> prepared to just <u>fade away</u> as he gets older. He wants to "drink / Life to the lees".

November (Pages 58-59)

1) The poet finds the <u>old people</u> depressing to look at — their "pasty bloodless smiles" make them seem <u>almost dead</u> already.
2) He realises that he and John will soon be <u>old</u> too — "we are almost these monsters".
3) The thought of growing old <u>scares</u> him witless — "we feel the terror of the dusk begin."
4) He knows there's <u>nothing</u> he can do to avoid getting old and dying, but says it's important to <u>make the most</u> out of the times when "we feel alive".

"Oh no! I'm going to die!"

This page is dedicated to Adrian Mole Aged 13 and ¾...

Other poems about getting older are: 'Before You Were Mine' (p.44-45) and 'My father thought it bloody queer' (p.54-55). That's it for poets' ideas, attitudes and feelings. Phew.

Strong Emotions

Poets often show strong emotions in their poems — either their own emotions, or those of the people they are writing about. Strong emotions are things like love, hate, anger, jealousy and joy.

1) Poems are often about <u>personal</u> subjects, which the poet has strong emotions about.

2) Poems about <u>difficult situations</u> often contain strong emotions, e.g. poems about death or danger.

3) Poets can show strong emotions through the <u>language they use</u> to write about a subject.

4) When a poet writes about strong emotions, it can make the reader think about times when they felt the same way. It often increases the <u>connection</u> the reader feels to the poem.

Poems about Difficult Situations show Strong Emotions

On my first Sonne (Pages 6-7)

1) The poet <u>loved</u> his son and was very <u>proud</u> of him — he calls him his "best piece of poetrie".

2) He's <u>devastated</u> by his son's death, but he's also <u>grateful</u> for the time he had with him — "Seven yeeres tho'wert lent to me and I thee pay."

3) Jonson sees life as <u>painful</u>. He suggests people are <u>better off dead</u>, as they don't have to suffer the pain of getting old — he asks: "why / Will man lament the state he should envie?"

Tichborne's Elegy (Pages 14-15)

1) This poem was written as the poet was <u>waiting for his execution</u> in the Tower of London.

2) The poet feels huge <u>sadness</u> and <u>bitterness</u> about his coming execution.

3) Throughout the poem, he keeps pointing out the <u>bitter irony</u> of his situation: even though he is young and healthy, his life is coming to an end: "My fruit is fallen, and yet my leaves are green".

4) He feels <u>angry</u> about the way his life is going to be <u>wasted</u>. Instead of being able to enjoy his life, it's going to be cut short: "My prime of youth is but a frost of cares."

Poems can Include Mixed Emotions

Havisham (Pages 36-37)

1) Havisham has very strong <u>mixed emotions</u> about the man who jilted her, calling him "Beloved sweetheart bastard".

2) She's extremely <u>angry</u> and <u>bitter</u>, and wants to "strangle" him.

3) It's years since he rejected her, but she <u>can't let go</u> — "I stink and remember." She's <u>obsessed</u>.

4) Behind all the violence, she's also very <u>unhappy</u>, wondering "who did this / to me?"

5) She also desperately wants him to be there, and has <u>sexual fantasies</u> about "the lost body".

November (Pages 58-59)

1) This poem describes an elderly woman being taken to a care home. The poet feels <u>guilty</u> about putting the woman into care: "We have brought her here to die and we know it."

2) The poet's <u>feelings</u> about the elderly people in the care home are <u>mixed</u>.

3) On the one hand, the poet seems <u>repulsed</u> by the elderly people, describing them as almost <u>inhuman</u>. For example, he describes their "pasty bloodless smiles" and their "stunned brains".

4) But the poet can also <u>empathise</u> with the elderly people — he can <u>imagine growing old himself</u>, and realises it's only a matter of time before he ends up in the same situation.

5) He sounds <u>frightened</u> and <u>depressed</u> by old age, and the fact that he can do nothing to stop it happening. Nightfall is used as a <u>metaphor</u> for old age: "we let it happen. We can say nothing."

Strong emotions are dramatic and compelling...

Poems are often about personal or dramatic events — no wonder they're emotional.
'The Affliction of Margaret' (p.10-11) and 'Kid' (p.60-61) are also good examples of this theme.

Use of the First Person

If the poet writes in the <u>first person</u>, they use words like "<u>I</u>" and "<u>me</u>", rather than "she" and "him."

> 1) Writing in the first person allows the poet to use their voice <u>directly</u>.
> 2) This allows them to talk about their personal <u>thoughts and feelings</u>.
> 3) The first person lets us see things from the poet or character's <u>point of view</u>.

Writing in the First Person can Express Personal Feelings

Anne Hathaway (Pages 40-41)

1) The poet imagines Anne Hathaway's <u>feelings</u> after her husband dies.
2) The use of the first person makes the poem sound <u>loving</u> and <u>tender</u> — for example when she says, "My lover's words / were shooting stars" and "My living laughing love".
3) Using the first person emphasises how <u>personal</u> the poem is. It's about memories of a relationship — the kind of stuff other people wouldn't know about.

My father thought it bloody queer (Pages 54-55)

1) The poet uses the first person to show the <u>physical pain</u> he felt from having his ear pierced, and the <u>emotional pain</u> caused by his father's reaction.
2) He says he <u>hadn't dared</u> to "drive a needle through the skin". This shows he wasn't very courageous about it, and makes his attempt to be rebellious look a bit <u>silly</u>.
3) He shows that his father's mocking reaction <u>still bothers him</u>, as he describes "my own voice breaking like a tear" when he finds himself saying the same things his dad said to him.

Sonnet (Pages 34-35)

1) This poem is about how much the poet loves the <u>countryside in summer</u>.
2) Three lines of the poem start with "<u>I love</u>" which emphasises his feelings.

Writing in the First Person can be Persuasive

The Man He Killed (Pages 16-17)

1) This poem makes a point about the <u>barbarity and foolishness of war</u> — how people who could be friends kill each other because they are on different sides.
2) Hardy writes in the first person from the <u>point of view of a soldier</u> who has fought in a war. This <u>increases the impact</u> of the message because the character is speaking from <u>personal experience</u>.
3) Using the first person makes it sound as if the character is <u>talking directly</u> to the reader: "I shot him dead because – / Because he was my foe". This makes the poem more <u>compelling</u> and <u>persuasive</u>.

The Song of the Old Mother (Pages 8-9)

1) The message of the poem is about how <u>harsh</u> life is for many <u>old people</u>.
2) The poet writes in the first person, from the point of view of an old woman.
3) The character of the woman <u>talks directly to the reader</u> about her situation. She describes her <u>list of chores</u>, starting early "in the dawn" and not stopping till the "stars" are out. She contrasts this with the "idleness" of young people.
4) The poem gives a voice to a character who would <u>usually be ignored</u>.

The first person lets the poet speak directly to the reader...

'Stealing' (p.50-51) and 'Mother, any distance' (p.52-53) also use the first person. It makes a big difference to the effect of a poem, as it lets the poet talk personally — poems like 'The Man He Killed' would <u>lose a lot of impact</u> if it was just "he" or "she" instead of "I".

Characters

Most poets write about people — apart from the nature-loving, obsessed-with-potatoes brigade.

> 1) Many poems are about a particular character — their <u>personality</u>, <u>actions</u> and <u>emotions</u>.
>
> 2) The characters in a poem can be <u>real</u> or completely <u>made-up</u>.
>
> 3) Sometimes the main character is the <u>poet</u> themselves.
>
> 4) Often an important character isn't actually present in the poem — they're just <u>talked about</u> by the other characters.

Characters can be Portrayed Negatively

Kid (Pages 60-61)

1) The poem is addressed to a character who was a <u>father-figure</u> to the poet in his childhood.
2) The poet says that he hero-worshipped this character but was <u>badly let down</u> by him — ditched "in the gutter".
3) Even now the poet is older, he's <u>still bitter</u> about the way he was treated. He enjoys thinking about the character being unhappy and alone: "punching the palm of your hand all winter".
4) He refers to the character <u>sarcastically</u> as "<u>Batman, big-shot</u>". He used to think the character was a big hero, but it turned out he was much more ordinary.

Havisham (Pages 36-37)

1) The character in this poem is based on a character called <u>Miss Havisham</u>, in Charles Dickens' novel "<u>Great Expectations</u>". She was jilted on her wedding day and went a bit <u>crazy</u>.
2) In the poem, she has extremely <u>violent</u> thoughts about the bloke who rejected her, but she's also <u>desperate</u> for him to come back. She's <u>obsessed</u> with the rejection she suffered.
3) We can see her <u>confusion</u> in the opening line, when she calls him "Beloved sweetheart bastard."
4) Overall, she's very <u>bitter</u> and <u>violent</u> — her grim request of "a male corpse for a long slow honeymoon" shows she's lost control.

Sometimes a Key Character is Absent

The Affliction of Margaret (Pages 10-11)

1) In this poem, a woman called Margaret worries about what has happened to her son who disappeared seven years ago. Even though we <u>never meet the son</u>, he is an <u>important character</u> in the poem.
2) Margaret's opinion of her son is very <u>loving and positive</u>. She says that he was "among the prime in worth, / An object beauteous to behold".
3) There are hints though, that her son <u>wasn't perfect</u>. She says, "if things ensued that wanted grace, / As hath been said, they were not base". This suggests that other people didn't like his behaviour — but Margaret still defends him.

My Last Duchess (Pages 22-23)

1) In the poem, a rich man looks at a painting of his <u>dead wife</u> and describes what she was like.
2) The <u>character</u> of the dead wife is described in a lot of detail — but all through the <u>eyes of her husband</u>, who had her <u>killed</u>. We never hear her side of the story.
3) The husband says his wife made him angry because she favoured everyone with her <u>smiles and blushes</u>, rather than saving them for him. There is a suggestion that she was <u>unfaithful</u> to him: "she liked whate'er / She looked on, and her looks went everywhere."

Characters are just the people in a poem...

Other poems with interesting characters include: 'Ulysses' (p.26-27), 'The Village Schoolmaster' (p.28-29), 'Salome' (p.42-43), 'Education for Leisure' (p.48-49) and 'Hitcher' (p.66-67).

Imagery

The way a poet writes can make you form a picture in your head of what's being described — this is called "imagery". Two common forms of imagery are <u>metaphors</u> and <u>similes</u> (see glossary).

> 1) Imagery helps the reader <u>imagine</u> the situations, characters and emotions described in a poem.
>
> 2) Imagery often uses <u>comparisons</u> to describe something, e.g. "She ran like the wind."

Imagery can be used to Describe People

I've made out a will (Pages 64-65)

1) The poet gives a lot of fairly <u>disgusting</u> but <u>humorous</u> descriptions of the <u>insides</u> of his <u>body</u>.
2) The "jellies and tubes and syrups and glues" sound pretty <u>horrible</u>. They make it sound like his body is made up of <u>food</u>, with "bilberry soup" in his veins instead of <u>blood</u>.
3) The <u>skeleton</u> is described as "the chassis or cage or cathedral of bone" — this gives an idea of it being a big <u>structure</u>, like a car or a building.
4) In lines 9-12, the poet describes his body as if it's a <u>shop</u>, an <u>engine</u>, <u>clothes</u> and a <u>clock</u>. Describing his heart as "the pendulum, the ticker" gives the impression that when he <u>dies</u>, it'll just be like when a <u>clock stops ticking</u>.

Before

Before You Were Mine (Pages 44-45)

1) The poet uses imagery to describe the life her <u>mother</u> had, before she was born.
2) The <u>images</u> are quite <u>nostalgic</u> — her mum playing on a street corner, staying out late and dancing. These are things she wouldn't do in the same way again, once she settled down and had kids.
3) She uses <u>glamorous language</u> to describe her mother's younger self: "Marilyn", "fizzy, movie tomorrows", "high-heeled red shoes", "scent", "sparkle". This creates an image of a <u>fun-loving young girl</u>, full of ideals and <u>dreams</u>.

After

Some Poets use Imagery to Describe Places

Patrolling Barnegat (Pages 18-19)

1) The poet describes watchmen patrolling the beach during a <u>fierce storm</u>. He uses imagery to create a sense of how strong and frightening the storm is.
2) He describes the bad weather as if it is a <u>violent, attacking force</u> — e.g. "savagest trinity lashing".
3) The <u>sound of the gale</u> is described as if it's a <u>person's voice</u>: there's an "incessant undertone muttering" and sometimes it sounds like someone shrieking with "demoniac laughter".
4) He emphasises the <u>gloominess</u> of the scene with words like "midnight", "shadows" and "murk".

Inversnaid (Pages 32-33)

1) The poet describes a place he loves in the <u>countryside</u>. He makes an appeal for wild, natural places to be left as they are.
2) He builds up an image of the "<u>darksome burn</u>" in the first three verses. He emphasises the <u>colours</u>: the river is "horseback brown", the lake "pitchblack" and the froth on the lake "fawn".
3) He also describes the <u>movement</u> of the place: the river "roaring down" to the lake, the froth "turns and twindles" over the water, the brook "treads through" the hills.

Imagery is an important poetic device...

Most poems have a bit of imagery in. It's a useful way for a poet to give a particular impression of something. Examples include: 'Anne Hathaway' (p.40-41), 'Mother, any distance' (p.52-53), 'Homecoming' (p.56-57), 'The Eagle' (p.24-25), 'Ulysses' (p.26-27) and 'Sonnet' (p.34-35).

Closing Couplets

A closing couplet is the last two lines of a poem.

1) A closing couplet can sum up the poem as a whole.
2) A closing couplet can make a new or surprising point, giving the poem an unexpected conclusion.
3) Closing couplets can be set apart from the rest of the poem, and sometimes they rhyme.

Closing Couplets can Sum Up a Poem

The Village Schoolmaster (Pages 28-29)

1) The closing couplet seems to sum up the poem, by telling us how the villagers were baffled by how much the schoolmaster knew.
2) There is some uncertainty too. "Still the wonder grew" could mean that the villagers are impressed by the schoolmaster — but it might suggest that they aren't sure what to make of him. They seem amused by him, rather than in awe of him.

"Still the wonder grew"

I've made out a will (Pages 64-65)

1) The last two lines are separate from the rest of the poem. This emphasises the point they make.
2) The poem lists the parts of the poet's body that he's happy to leave to the NHS.
3) But the closing couplet says they can't have his heart — "not the pendulum, the ticker". The poet uses these two lines to make his wishes absolutely clear.

Closing Couplets can be Surprising

Sonnet 130 (Pages 20-21)

1) Shakespeare seems to be criticising his mistress, but the last two lines show he does love her really.
2) The closing couplet surprises the reader. It makes us look at the rest of the poem in a different way.
3) His love seems all the more genuine because he knows she's not perfect — "I think my love as rare / As any she belied with false compare."

November (Pages 58-59)

1) Most of this poem has a fairly depressing tone — the poet sees the old people in the home and they make him think about how his own death is unavoidable.
2) In the closing couplet, the poet is a bit more positive. He says "the sun spangles" — he sees a ray of light and feels more hopeful when he thinks of the times that "we feel alive".
3) The poet concludes that people should make the most out of opportunities when they come up — "One thing we have to get, John, out of this life."

Closing couplets leave a lasting impression on the reader...

Other poems with interesting closing couplets are: 'Anne Hathaway' (p.40-41), 'Salome' (p.42-43), 'Hitcher' (p.66-67), 'On my first Sonne' (p.6-7), 'The Song of the Old Mother (p.8-9) and 'Tichborne's Elegy' (p.14-15). Remember to write about how they relate to the rest of the poem.

Irony

Irony can be <u>funny</u>, but it can also be <u>tragic</u>.

> 1) It's ironic when <u>words</u> are used in a <u>sarcastic</u> or <u>comic</u> way to <u>imply the opposite</u> of what they normally mean. People often do this to draw attention to something being funny or odd.
>
> 2) It's ironic when there is a big <u>difference</u> between what people <u>expect or hope for</u> and <u>what actually happens</u>.

Sometimes the Whole Poem is Ironic

Tichborne's Elegy (Pages 14-15)

1) The <u>irony</u> in this poem is that even though the poet is still <u>young</u> and <u>healthy</u>, his life is <u>almost over</u> because he is about to be executed: "My youth is spent, and yet I am not old".

2) Tichborne <u>repeats</u> this idea throughout the poem, with each line making clear the <u>bitter irony</u> of his situation: "And now I live, and now my life is done."

The Man He Killed (Pages 16-17)

1) The poet points out that the man he <u>shot dead</u> could have been his <u>friend</u> if they'd met in <u>different circumstances</u>.

2) It's ironic that, if they'd met "By some old and ancient inn", rather than being lined up opposite each other across a battlefield, they would have been <u>having a drink</u> together instead of <u>shooting at each other</u>.

Kid (Pages 60-61)

1) Robin <u>sarcastically</u> calls Batman a "big shot" — people used to think Batman was a big <u>hero</u>.

2) Now things have <u>changed</u>. Robin's the "real boy wonder" and Batman's <u>lonely</u> and <u>poor</u> — Robin pictures Batman "stewing over / chicken giblets in the pressure cooker".

3) It seems <u>ironic</u> that things have turned out this way, and Robin takes <u>pleasure</u> in pointing out this irony: "Batman, it makes a <u>marvellous picture</u>".

Irony Can Come Out at the End of the Poem

Salome (Pages 42-43)

1) This poem has lots of words which seem to have perfectly <u>innocent</u> meanings at first, but seem a lot more <u>sinister</u> when we find out what has actually happened at the end of the poem.

2) The man's "rather matted" hair and "crimson mouth" turn out to be like that because the woman has <u>killed</u> him — they're covered in <u>blood</u>.

3) The phrase "ain't life a bitch" is said <u>ironically</u> — the character doesn't really care about the dead man.

Those bastards in their mansions (Pages 62-63)

1) The character in the poem says he's <u>innocent</u> of all the things he's been <u>accused</u> of — he hasn't "poisoned the dogs", "crossed the lawns" or "given heat and light to streets and houses".

2) Rather than daringly stirring up a <u>revolution</u>, he says: "I stick to the shadows, carry a <u>gun</u>."

3) The <u>irony</u> is that he's actually planning something a lot more <u>serious</u> than the things he's denying. This irony only becomes clear in the <u>last line</u> of the poem.

Isn't it ironic...

Here are some other poems that have irony in them: 'Elvis's Twin Sister', (p.38-39), 'We Remember Your Childhood Well' (p.46-47), 'My father thought it bloody queer' (p.54-55), 'Hitcher' (p.66-67), 'My Last Duchess' (p.22-23) and 'The Laboratory' (p.30-31).

Language Effects

Language effects are the way the sounds of words in a poem are used to make a certain impression on the reader. Examples of language effects are alliteration, rhyme, assonance and onomatopoeia.

1) Language effects can create a mood or atmosphere in a poem.

2) Language effects can be useful for creating a vivid picture in the reader's mind of the place or person described in the poem.

3) Language effects can make a poet's feelings or opinions more forceful and convincing.

Language Effects Can be Used to Describe Nature

Patrolling Barnegat (Pages 18-19)

1) There's half-rhyme throughout the poem, with each line ending with a verb with an "-ing" ending. These are mostly words to do with the movement of the wind and sea, e.g. "lashing", "careering", and this creates a fearsome, unrelenting feel to the storm.

2) The poet uses onomatopoeic words to create the effect of the sounds of the storm, e.g. the vowel sounds of "hoarse roar" remind us of the deep rumbling sounds of a fierce storm.

3) Alliteration of hard "c" sounds in "combs careering" makes the sea sound rough and dangerous.

Inversnaid (Pages 32-33)

1) Alliteration in the phrase "rollrock highroad roaring" makes the reader think of the roar of the water flowing down over the stony bed of the stream.

2) The harsh alliteration of "in coop and in comb" adds to the impression of a rugged setting.

3) Rhyming couplets and a regular rhythm give the poem a natural and attractive feel.

4) In the last verse, the poet makes a point about how important it is to keep places like Inversnaid as they are. By repeating "w" sounds, the poet makes his point more effective, reminding us of the sounds of the countryside, like the wind blowing around the hills.

Language Effects Can be Used to Describe Feelings

Stealing (Pages 50-51)

1) The alliteration of "m" sounds in lines 2-4 creates an excited feel — the character is telling a story that they think is interesting.

2) The rhyming words in the poem show how the character sees certain things as being connected, e.g. "head" and "dead".

3) The irregularity of the rhyming shows how the character's thoughts jump about fairly randomly — he/she seems rather unstable.

Kid (Pages 60-61)

1) Every line in the poem rhymes or half-rhymes, e.g. "order", "wander", "yonder", "rather". This gives the poem a relentless feel, reflecting Robin's accusing, sometimes mocking tone.

2) The repeated, heavy rhythm in "taller, harder, stronger, older" emphasises how much Robin has changed. This adds to the aggressive, defiant feel.

3) Alliteration in "next to nothing" and "punching the palm" make Robin's vision of Batman's downfall seem more dramatic and hard-hitting.

Language effects make descriptions more memorable...

Think about the effect each poet is trying to create. You could write about the language effects in these poems: 'The Eagle' (p.24-25), 'Sonnet' (p.34-35), 'Salome' (p.42-43) and 'Those bastards in their mansions' (p.62-63).

Mood

Mood is the <u>feel</u> or <u>atmosphere</u> of a poem. There are loads of different kinds of mood, e.g. light-hearted, tense, comical, threatening.

> 1) Mood can be created by describing a particular <u>setting</u>.
> 2) Poets can create a certain mood by describing <u>feelings</u> — their own or other people's.
> 3) The mood can <u>change</u> from one part of a poem to another.

Mood can Come from the Situation

Sonnet (Pages 34-35)

1) The poet creates a <u>peaceful</u>, <u>happy</u> mood. The poem starts with "I love", so it starts on a <u>positive</u> note.
2) There are lots of <u>idyllic countryside images</u>, such as the "willow leaning half way o'er / The clear deep lake". These descriptions give the poem a <u>tranquil</u> feel.
3) There's plenty of <u>colour</u> too, which gives the feel of a bright, carefree summer's day.
4) The insects' "happy wings" and the description of the beetles playing make the scene seem <u>carefree</u> and <u>natural</u>.

Tichborne's Elegy (Pages 14-15)

Bitter, Chidiock?

1) The mood in this poem is <u>sad</u>, <u>regretful</u> and rather <u>bitter</u>.
2) Tichborne talks about how he's still <u>young</u> and fit, but his life will soon be <u>over</u> when he's <u>executed</u>. He seems <u>bitter</u> about his fate — "My feast of joy is but a dish of pain".
3) The poet constantly points out the <u>bitter irony</u> of his situation. The whole poem has a <u>miserable</u>, <u>desperate tone</u>.

Uncertainty can Create a Sinister Mood

We Remember Your Childhood Well (Pages 46-47)

1) This poem has an <u>unpleasant</u>, <u>sinister</u> mood. The person whose voice we hear makes a string of <u>denials</u>, suggesting that something <u>very nasty</u> has gone on in the past.
2) We don't hear directly what's being denied, which adds to the <u>dark tone</u>. The phrase "Nobody hurt you" hints at <u>child abuse</u> of some kind.
3) The person talking tries to <u>confuse</u> the person who's made the accusations — "The moment's a blur". This makes us <u>distrust</u> them, as they seem to be <u>covering things up</u>, and they don't offer clear explanations.
4) The mood becomes even <u>bleaker</u> at the end of the poem. The "skidmarks of sin" suggest how <u>horrible</u> the past events must have been.

Homecoming (Pages 56-57)

1) The first line sets the tone for a <u>mysterious</u> poem: "Think, two things on their own and both at once". The poet challenges us, as well as the woman he's talking to, to <u>figure out</u> how the "canary-yellow cotton jacket" and the trust exercise are related.
2) There's a <u>tense</u> mood in this poem, as it's <u>difficult</u> to work out exactly what's going on and how the things described in the poem are <u>connected</u> to each other.
3) There's also <u>tension</u> between the person the poet is talking to and her mother — "You seeing red. Blue murder. Bed."
4) The "<u>silhouette</u>" of a man who "wants to <u>set things straight</u>" seems <u>threatening</u>.

You'll probably never be in the mood for an exam...

Good poems to look at for this theme include: 'On my first Sonne' (p.6-7), 'The Affliction of Margaret' (p.10-11), 'Havisham' (p.36-37), 'Elvis's Twin Sister' (p.38-39) and 'Hitcher' (p.66-67).

Stage 1 — Planning

Before you write the essay, you've got to plan it. Spend ten minutes planning — that leaves you with fifty minutes for writing. Use this two-stage method to plan your essay:

A Read the Question Carefully and Underline Key Words

1) Read the question you've chosen a couple of times. The question will usually ask you how the poems show/present/use/convey the theme. Underline the theme and any other important words.

2) You have to compare four poems altogether. The question will give you the titles of one or two poems that you have to write about. You'll get some choice about which other poems you're going to compare. Pick poems which relate to the theme in the question.

3) Look up the poems you're going to write about in the copy of the Anthology you are given in the exam. Bend the corner over on those pages, so that you can find them again quickly.

EXAMPLE QUESTION

They want you to compare the poems.

The theme of this question is characters.

Question 1   Compare the ways characters are portrayed in *Havisham* by Carol Ann Duffy, *Kid* by Simon Armitage and two poems from the Pre-1914 Poetry Bank.

This bit tells you which poems to use in your answer.

B Spend 5-10 minutes Planning your Essay

Write a plan at the top of your answer paper — this will help you write a good essay. Just scribble stuff down, like in the example below. At the end of the exam, draw a neat line through your plan, so the examiner knows that it's rough work. Here's an example:

Plan: poems to write about: Ulysses, The Village Schoolmaster, Havisham, Kid

1) Intro about theme - characters

2) Structure
Ulysses: 4 verses, each shows diff emotion
Village: 1 verse, descriptions blend together
Havisham: verses flow into each other
Kid: similar to Village Schoolmaster

3) Language
Ulysses: frustrated, heroic
Village: nostalgic, mysterious
Havisham: aggressive, confused
Kid: vengeful, sarcastic

4) Attitudes and feelings
Ulysses: boredom, pride, excitement
Village: respect, fear
Havisham: bitterness, loneliness
Kid: revenge

5) Conclusion - personal response:
Liked Ulysses because you see his human side

Planning is the basis of a good essay...

Always write a plan. It'll help you get your ideas in order, and write a well-structured essay. Once you've got a plan, you know what you're going to write — it will give you confidence.

Stage 2 — Writing

Now you've planned your essay, you've got to write it.
Follow this five-step method for a brilliant essay every time.

For advice about two-part questions, see pages 86-87.

⟨1⟩ *Write about the Theme in the Introduction*

1) Give a definition. It doesn't have to be detailed — just describe what you think the theme means.
2) Explain how the theme is explored in the poems you will write about.

⟨2⟩ *Compare the Structure of Each Poem*

1) Say how the structure of the poems relates to the theme of the question.
   For ideas, look at the 'What Happens in the Poem' parts of the pages on each poem.
2) Write about the similarities and differences between the structures of the poems.
3) You could write about some of these things, if any of them really stand out:

• Line length	• Rhyme or rhythm	• Symmetry	• Punctuation
• Stanza shape	• Repetition	• Narrative or time scale	• Layout

⟨3⟩ *Compare the Use of Language in the Poems*

1) Write about how the language of the poems relates to the theme of the question.
   For ideas, look at the 'Types of Language' parts of the pages on each poem.
2) Write about the similarities and differences in the way language is used in the poems.
3) You could write about some of these things, if any of them really stand out:

• Images, similes and metaphors	• Onomatopoeia	• Personification	• Questions or commands
• Who is speaking	• Alliteration	• Non-standard English	• Tone or atmosphere

⟨4⟩ *Compare the Feelings and Attitudes in the Poems*

1) Write about how these feelings and attitudes relate to the theme.
   For ideas, look at the 'Feeling and Attitudes' parts of the pages on each poem.
2) Write about the similarities and differences between the feelings and attitudes in the poems.

⟨5⟩ *Give a Personal Response to the Poems in the Conclusion*

1) Say which poem you preferred and why.
2) Show some empathy — connect the poem to your own feelings and experiences.

And finally — don't forget to check through your work...

We've included some 'A' grade essay answers on the next few pages. They use the
method described here and should give you a good idea of what you're aiming for...

Sample Essay — Death

Here's another example of a typical exam question — and how to answer it well...

A Here's an Exam-style Question about Death

Question 1   You should answer both (a) and (b).

(a)   Compare how death is presented in *Hitcher* by Simon Armitage and one poem by Carol Ann Duffy.

(b)   Compare how death is presented in *The Laboratory* by Robert Browning and one other poem from the Pre-1914 Poetry Bank.

B Here's an Example of a Plan for this Answer

Plan: poems to write about: Salome, Hitcher, The Man He Killed, The Laboratory

(a) 1) Intro about theme – death

2) Structure

Salome: Only reveals murder at end of poem, clues

Hitcher: Also starts off normal, then murder

3) Language

Sal: humour, casual tone, first person

Hit: contrast ordinary life / violence, humour, fp

4) Attitudes and feelings

Sal: evil, pride in killing almost, bored of it

Hit: cold, distant, pride

5) Conclusion

Both show death from murderer's point of view.

(b) 1) Intro

2) Structure

Man he killed: short poem, message at end

Laboratory: long, 12 stanzas, scattered thoughts

3) Language

Man: colloquial, likeable, fp

Lab: melodramatic, excited, fp

4) Attitudes and feelings

Man: irony, empathy

Lab: revenge, evil

5) Conclusion

Strong contrast

Here's an 'A' Grade Answer to the Question

Intro. 1

(a) Death is an emotional subject, often connected to feelings of grief, sadness and loss. The poems 'Salome' and 'Hitcher' are unusual in that they instead present death as mundane and humorous. Both poems are written in the first person, from the point of view of a murderer. These characters don't experience the usual emotions associated with death and are unrepentant about killing.

Treat each part of the question, (a) and (b), like a mini-essay.

Structure 2

The structures of the poems are important in the ways the poets present death. In both poems, we don't realise at first that the narrator is a murderer. In 'Salome' the implication is that the narrator has woken up after a drunken one night stand: "woke up with a head on the pillow beside me — whose — ?" Only in the last stanza is it revealed that she has beheaded the man. Likewise, in 'Hitcher' the narrator seems fairly ordinary at the start of the poem. The narrator describes feeling "tired, under / the weather". It is only in the third stanza that the reader suddenly realises that the narrator is a murderer.

Remember to relate the structure of the poems to the theme.

The key words in the question are highlighted in green.

Lang. 3

The way the poets use language to describe death is slightly different in 'Salome' and 'Hitcher'. In 'Salome', there is a humorous tone throughout the poem. The narrator's voice is lively and jokey, for example when she says the man she woke up next to was "Good-looking, of course". Even when she reveals the

Give examples and quotes from the poems to back up your points.

THIS IS A FLAP.
FOLD THIS PAGE OUT.

Sample Essay — Characters

1 Intro.

Characters are the people whose personalities, emotions or actions are portrayed in a poem. They can be real or fictional. Poets use various techniques to present their characters. In 'Ulysses', we see a heroic warrior who is determined to continue his adventures, whereas 'The Village Schoolmaster' is about a more ordinary character. The main character in 'Havisham' is a bitter, violent person, while in 'Kid' we see a young adult getting revenge on his neglectful guardian.

Briefly discuss the theme in the introduction.

2 Structure

The structure of the poems is related to how the characters are portrayed. The structure of 'Ulysses' consists of four verses of differing lengths. This allows Tennyson to show Ulysses' views about different aspects of his life: his frustration at ruling "a savage race", his determination to continue travelling, his feelings about his son Telemachus, and his motivational speech to his crew. In this way we get a good idea of Ulysses' overall character. In contrast, Goldsmith's poem, 'The Village Schoolmaster', is not divided into verses. As in 'Ulysses', different aspects of the character are described, such as his "severe" nature and his many skills, but these merge into each other fluently, rather than being separate. 'Havisham' by Duffy is divided into four verses of four lines each. However, they are not totally separate, as enjambment such as "Love's / hate" links the second, third and fourth verses together. This emphasises how unstable the character is, as some of the things she says don't seem to make sense at first. Armitage's poem 'Kid' has a similar structure to 'The Village Schoolmaster', consisting of one verse of 24 lines. This enables the narrator to gradually change our perception of the "Batman" character, who is sarcastically described as a "big shot" in the first line, but by the end is a miserable loner, with the narrator emerging as "the real boy wonder".

It's not enough just to write about the structure of the poems — you've got to say how it relates to the theme.

3 Language

In each poem, the style of language used affects our perception of the characters. Ulysses' speech is eloquent, whether he's frustrated, excited or proud. He is at his most impressive when he addresses his crew. He refers to them as "my friends", showing he knows them well, and we also see how brave he is, as, although he is old, he still vows to "sail beyond the sunset". In contrast, the uncertain language in 'The Village Schoolmaster' makes the character appear slightly mysterious, as if people were not quite sure what he was like. We are impressed by "The love he bore to learning", but phrases like "still the wonder grew" add to the general impression that the schoolmaster was a strange man.

Compare the way the poets have used language to present the theme.

The language used in 'Havisham' is aggressive but confused. The opening sentence, "Beloved sweetheart bastard" sets the tone for how the character's bitter violent feelings are interspersed with the sadness and loneliness she feels because of her rejection. Similarly, the language in 'Kid' shows the Robin character's bitterness, but it is more purposeful and coherent than that in 'Havisham'. Robin conjures a vivid image of Batman "stewing over / chicken giblets in the pressure cooker", and this brings his revenge against Batman to a neat conclusion.

Back up your points with quotes from the poems.

4 Feelings and Attitudes

The feelings and attitudes expressed in these poems also affect the way the characters come across. Ulysses experiences a range of feelings: boredom at the prospect of ruling his people, pride when he thinks of what he has "seen and known", and excitement at his coming travels. The feelings and attitudes in 'The Village Schoolmaster' are less obvious. The narrator seems to respect this character for his knowledge and skills, but he also says the schoolmaster was rather intimidating: the children, or "boding tremblers", had to pretend to find his jokes funny so as not to upset him.

The main emotions in 'Havisham' are intense bitterness and anger. The character is so set on revenge for her rejection that any "male corpse" will do. However, we also see glimpses of how lonely she is: she fantasises that "the lost body" is there in bed with her, and her awareness of what she has become — "who did this / to me?" — suggests she is still suffering from the heartbreak of rejection. Revenge is also a major theme in 'Kid', as the narrator gets his own back on the Batman character for neglecting him by revealing the truth about him. His sarcastic, tabloid-headline style remark, "Holy robin-redbreast-nest-egg-shocker", shows he is enjoying bringing Batman's reputation down.

Link the feelings and attitudes in the poem to the theme.

5 Conc.

These poems have an interesting and diverse range of characters. I particularly enjoyed the depiction of Ulysses. Tennyson makes this classical hero seem all the more impressive for the fact that he knows he is not as young and strong as he once was, yet he is still determined to "drink / Life to the lees". I find this truly admirable.

Give a personal response in the conclusion.

Sample Essay — Death

3 Language
gruesome death, there is still a strong vein of black humour: "there, like I said – and ain't life a bitch – / was his head on a platter." The language used in 'Hitcher' is bleaker. This is partly because the murder is described in detail: hitting the man "six times with the krooklok / in the face". The black humour in the poem ("I let him have it / on the top road out of Harrogate") adds to the impact of the murder.

4 Attitudes
The attitudes in the poems towards death are different. Salome shows an ambivalent attitude to death. She sounds almost bored with killing ("doubtless I'll do it again"), but she's also excited by it — her "eyes glitter" when she sees the blood and the dead man. In contrast, in 'Hitcher', the character's attitude towards death seems cold and unemotional. He seems to take pride in killing the man without losing control of the car: "didn't even swerve." The murder was premeditated as the character had hired a car. This contrasts with Salome, who killed drunkenly and impulsively.

5 Conc.
These poems both present death from the point of view of murderers. There is black humour and brutality in both poems. This makes them uneasy reading. I feel uncomfortable laughing at the humour in 'Hitcher', for example the phrase "I dropped it into third", because of the violence being described.

1 Intro.
(b) The poems 'The Man He Killed' and 'The Laboratory' present death in different ways. In 'The Man He Killed', a soldier describes killing a man in battle and the thoughts this stirred in him. In 'The Laboratory' a woman is planning a murder, possibly of her lover's new mistress.

2 Structure
The structure of the poems relates to how death is presented. 'The Man He Killed' is a short poem, containing a simple message about the tragedy of war, summed up in its final stanza: "You shoot a fellow down / You'd treat if met where any bar is". In contrast, in 'The Laboratory', there are numerous stanzas. These visualise the character's excitable, easily distracted frame of mind as she prepares for the murder.

3 Lang.
The poets also use language very differently to present death. The woman in 'The Laboratory' describes death in a cruelly melodramatic way: "He is sure to remember her dying face!". She asks lots of questions which makes her appear excited about the crime. In contrast, the character in 'The Man He Killed' uses plain language: "I shot at him as he at me". He killed in war, not out of malice.

4 Attitudes
The attitudes to death contrast greatly between the two poems. The character in 'The Man He Killed', killed out of duty. He can empathise with the man he killed ("just as I"), and sees the irony that they might have been friends in different circumstances. The woman in 'The Laboratory' has a very different attitude to death; she is excited by the thought of getting her revenge and causing pain: "Let death be felt". It gives her a sense of power over the people she imagines "laugh" at her.

5 Conc.
In conclusion, there is a strong contrast in the way these two poems present death. 'The Man He Killed' is a moving poem with a peaceful message. The line "No other reason why" makes me feel sad; the soldiers pitted against each other are fighting for no reason other than they needed a job. On the other hand, 'The Laboratory' shows a malicious, vengeful view of death.

Sample Essay — Imagery

Some of the exam questions will be about <u>poetic methods</u> e.g. imagery, first person, character. Don't be scared off by these questions — you can still answer them by looking at the structure, language and feelings/attitudes in the poems.

A Here's an Exam-style Question about Imagery

> **Question 1** Compare how imagery is used to create vivid descriptions in *Anne Hathaway* by Carol Ann Duffy and one poem by Simon Armitage. Then go on to compare the ways imagery is used in two of the poems from the Pre-1914 Poetry Bank.

B Here's an Example of a Plan for this Answer

Plan: poems to write about: Anne Hathaway, Mother any distance, Sonnet, The Eagle

1) Intro about theme — imagery

2) Structure
Anne Hath: sonnet form, 14 lines/rhyming end couplet
Mother any dist: almost sonnet, uneven line lengths

3) Language
Anne: romantic images, metaphor of language for love
Moth: images holding tape, still anchoring son who is moving away

4) Attitudes and feelings
Anne: joy in memories, fondness
Mother: still loves mum, needs independence

then go on to compare pre-1914 poems:

2) Structure
Sonnet: sonnet form, rhyme, repetition 'I love'
Eagle: short, rhythm, rhyme

3) Language
Sonnet: colour / shine, detailed description
Eagle: simile 'thunderbolt', image power/height

4) Attitudes and feelings
Sonnet: joy, happiness in small things
Eagle: power, respect for nature

5) Conclusion for whole essay
Preferred Anne

Here's an 'A' Grade Answer to the Question

Introduction

1 Imagery is the way poets use language to create vivid descriptions of situations, events and even emotions. In 'Anne Hathaway' by Carol Ann Duffy, imagery is used to show the narrator's fond, happy memories of her relationship with her late husband: the images are romantic and blissful. In 'Mother, any distance...' by Simon Armitage, imagery is also used to show the relationship between two characters, in this case the narrator and his mother. The two pre-1914 poems, 'The Eagle' by Alfred Tennyson and 'Sonnet' by John Clare use imagery differently. They both use imagery to describe nature, creating a vivid sense of its beauty.

Establish why the theme is important.

The key words in the question are highlighted in green.

Structure

2 'Anne Hathaway' is structured as a sonnet, with fourteen lines and a closing rhyming couplet. The sonnet form relates to the content and imagery in the poem: the narrator is describing her relationship with Shakespeare who was famous for his sonnets and breathtaking use of language. 'Mother, any distance...' also uses sonnet form as a basis for its structure, but changes and adapts it. For example, it isn't on the traditional fourteen lines, because the final phrase "to fall or fly" has been given its own line. This final phrase provides a strong image which sums up the feelings in the poem: it is given special emphasis by being put on its own.

This question asks for the Duffy/ Armitage poems to be compared first.

Sample Essay — Imagery

Both of these poems use language to create vivid imagery. In 'Anne Hathaway', there are romantic images, reminiscent of Shakespeare plays like 'Twelfth Night', to describe the couple's relationship: a fantasy world of "forest, castles, torchlight, clifftops, seas". Language is used as a metaphor for love: "my body now a softer rhyme / to his". The narrator uses this metaphor to show how in awe she was of the power of Shakespeare's writing. She imagines herself as a figment of his imagination: "I dream'd he had written me". 'Mother, any distance...' uses imagery to portray a different kind of relationship. The narrator describes walking up the stairs with a tape measure, with his mum holding the other end: "your fingertips still pinch / the last one-hundreth of an inch." There comes a point when he reaches the very top of the house, when she might have to let go. This image represents the narrator reaching a point in life where he needs to be independent from his mother and take risks: "to fall or fly."

The images in 'Anne Hathaway' and 'Mother, any distance...' are striking because they combine the everyday with the extraordinary. An old bed is described with the romance of "shooting stars" and "torchlight". A day spent measuring a new house is described in surreal terms: the "prairies of the floors" and a "space-walk". The poets' use of imagery emphasises how these ordinary objects and situations had special significance. 'Anne Hathaway' uses imagery to describe the uncommon joy the narrator associates with the bed: "The bed we loved in was a spinning world". In 'Mother, any distance...', the imagery shows the narrator's desire for independence. This feels strange and risky to him at first: "a hatch that opens on an endless sky".

The second part of this essay will compare the use of imagery in two pre-1914 poems: 'The Eagle' and 'Sonnet'. The structure of these poems relates to their use of imagery. 'The Eagle' is a very short poem, describing a single, striking image of an eagle perched on a crag before swooping on its prey. In a similar way, 'Sonnet' is quite a short poem with a single subject being described: the beauty of summer.

The imagery used in 'The Eagle' emphasises the bird's power and authority. The eagle is described as high up, looking down on the world from his "mountain walls": even the sea seems small and insignificant from his perch. The bird is described as almost human: he has "crookèd hands" not claws. The simile of a "thunderbolt" is used to describe the awe-inspiring force of the bird as it swoops for prey. In 'Sonnet' John Clare also uses imagery to describe the beauty of nature. However, he focuses on a tamer, softer side of nature: "wild flowers", "wool sack clouds" and "hay grass". He uses language to create an image of happiness: "beaming forth", "sport about", "happy wings", "play". In both poems, colour is used to accentuate the beauty of the scene: the "azure" sea in 'The Eagle' and "stain with gold the meadow" in 'Sonnet'.

The imagery Tennyson uses in 'The Eagle' shows his feelings of respect for nature and the beauty of the world. He describes a natural environment of sea, cliffs and sun, untouched by humans. 'Sonnet' is different because it focuses on the poet's enjoyment of nature: he repeats the phrase "I love" three times in the poem, joyously affirming his reaction to the scene he is describing.

All these poems use imagery to create vivid descriptions of their different subjects: love, growing up, nature's power and nature's beauty. I particularly like the way imagery is used to describe love in 'Anne Hathaway'. The phrase, "a verb dancing in the centre of a noun" describes the narrator's happiness in a witty and vibrant way.

Side notes:
- Back up your points with quotes.
- Compare the poets use of language.
- Talk about how the poets use the theme to show feelings and attitudes.
- Be careful to leave time to write about all four essays.
- Explain the different methods the poet has used to create an overall image.
- Keep comparing the poems all the way through.
- Always put in a conclusion.

Margin labels: Language 3 | Feelings and Attitudes 4 | Structure 2 | Language 3 | Feelings 4 | Conc. 5

Sample Essay — Parent/Child Relationships

Read through this sample answer for some <u>handy tips</u> on how to write a fantastic essay.
<u>Key words</u> have been highlighted in green — both in the question and the answer.

A Here's an Exam-style Question about Parent/Child Relationships

Question 1   Compare the ways parent/child relationships are presented in *Before You Were Mine* by Carol Ann Duffy and three other poems, one by Simon Armitage and any two from the Pre-1914 Poetry Bank.

B Here's an Example of a Plan for this Answer

<u>Plan:</u> poems to write about: Affliction of Margaret, On my First Sonne, My Father, Before You Were Mine

1) Intro about theme – parent/child relationships

2) Structure
Affliction: each verse shows diff state of mind
First Sonne: one verse, sums up feelings
Before: each verse about diff time (ish)
My father: each verse about diff event (ish)

3) Language
Affliction: extreme words/metaphors show strong feelings
Sonne: gentler, calmer language
Before: conversational language shows empathy with mum
My father: colloquial language makes it sound normal

4) Attitudes and feelings
Affliction: despair, sadness
First Sonne: sadness, acceptance, pride
Before: admiration, guilt
My father: pain

5) Conclusion - personal response:
I find On my first Sonne very moving
— "best piece of poetrie"

Here's an 'A' Grade Answer to the Question

Introduction
1   The relationship between a parent and a child can bring about any of a range of emotions. In 'The Affliction of Margaret', we see a parent's desperation at not hearing from her missing son in seven years, while in 'On my first Sonne', the poet bids farewell to his dead son. In 'Before You Were Mine', the poet describes the effect her own birth had on the lifestyle of her mother, whereas 'My father thought it bloody queer' describes a strained relationship between father and son.

Start by talking about the theme.

Structure
   The differing structures of the poems affect their impact. Wordsworth's structure for 'The Affliction of Margaret' consists of eleven verses of seven lines each, one for each year her son has been missing. Each verse shows a different aspect of Margaret's desperation to hear from her child, e.g. in the first verse she appeals for him to "find me, prosperous or undone!"; in the second verse she recalls the doomed glimpses of hope she's had: "I catch at them, and then I miss". This gives the impression that her state of mind changes from day to day.

Always keep the theme of the question in mind when you're talking about the structure of the poem.

2   The structure of 'On my first Sonne' is simpler than 'Affliction'. It consists of six rhyming couplets, making up just one verse in which Jonson, as a parent, pays tribute to his dead son. This makes the poem look like an inscription on a tombstone. Duffy's poem 'Before You Were Mine' also has a fairly regular structure, comprising four verses of five lines each, but with no regular rhyme scheme. Like 'Affliction', each verse describes a different thought, with the last verse describing the most recent thoughts.

Sample Essay — Parent/Child Relationships

Structure

2

The poem 'My father thought it bloody queer' by Armitage has a less regular structure than any of the three poems I have mentioned above. There are three verses, each with a different number of lines, and there is no regular rhyme scheme. As in 'The Affliction of Margaret' and 'Before You Were Mine', the effect of the verses is to separate the different ideas about the relationship between parent and child in the poem — the first verse describes his father's reaction to the earring, the second goes back to when he had his ear pierced, and the third describes how he now finds himself saying the same things as his father.

Talk about the effect created by the poems' structure.

There's only one part to this question, so compare all four poems throughout your essay.

Language

3

Each poet uses a different style of language to describe the parent/child relationship. In 'The Affliction of Margaret', there is a confused, obsessive style of language. Margaret often contradicts herself: "Neglect me! no I suffered long / from that ill thought". This shows her desperate state of mind. The language in 'On my first Sonne' is gentler and calmer. Jonson wants his son to "Rest in soft peace", and this expresses his tenderness towards his son and his acceptance that he has lost him.

'Before You Were Mine', on the other hand, uses conversational language to convey the idea that the poet is talking to her mother. Phrases such as "You reckon it's worth it" give the poem a personal feel and show that the poet is empathising with her mother. Similarly, 'My father' uses a conversational tone to show the relationship between son and father, although he does not address his parent directly. Colloquial phrases like "rolled home" give the poem a down-to-earth, everyday feel.

Say how the kind of language used affects the theme.

Use linking words and phrases like "similarly" and "in contrast".

Feelings and Attitudes

4

The attitudes towards parent/child relationships vary between the different poems. In 'Affliction', the breaking down of the relationship causes Margaret despair: the question "Was ever darkness like to this?" shows she cannot imagine a worse situation than the one she is in. Similarly, Jonson's feelings in 'On my first Sonne' are ones of sadness. However, the knowledge that his son is dead has allowed him to come to terms with what has happened; he says that perhaps death is the best state to be in, as his son has "scap'd worlds, and fleshes rage". He is also very proud of his son.

Feelings about parent/child relationships in the post-1914 poems are less clear cut. In 'Before You Were Mine', the poet admires her mother's rebellious life before she was born: she calls her "Marilyn", which shows she sees her as glamorous. However, the poet seems to think her own birth deprived her mother of this exciting life, forcing her to be responsible. In 'My father', the parent/child relationship is strained, as the father mocks the child for his attempt at rebellion. Now he has grown up, the poet finds himself saying the same things as his father, but we can see that the memory of his father's reaction still hurts, as he describes "my own voice breaking like a tear".

Remember to back up the points you make with relevant quotes.

Say how the feelings and attitudes in the poem are related to the theme.

Conclusion

5

All four of these poems take an interesting angle on the trials and tribulations of parent/child relationships. I feel that the most affecting is 'On my first Sonne'. I find this poem very moving, as Jonson bids a fond farewell to his son. He describes his son as his "best piece of poetrie", and I feel this is a beautiful way of showing the pride he had in his child.

Include a personal response to make the conclusion interesting.

Glossary

adjective	A word that <u>describes</u> something, e.g. "big", "fast", "annoying".
alliteration	Where words <u>start</u> with the <u>same letter</u>. It's often used in poetry to give a nice pattern to a phrase. E.g. 'Sally's slipper slipped on a slimy slug.'
ambiguity	Where a word or phrase has <u>two or more</u> possible <u>meanings</u>.
assonance	When words share the same vowel sound but the consonants are different. E.g. "Lisa had a p<u>ie</u>ce of ch<u>ee</u>se before sh<u>e</u> went to sl<u>ee</u>p, to help her dr<u>ea</u>m."
blank verse	Poetry that <u>doesn't rhyme</u>, usually in <u>iambic pentameters</u>.
colloquial	Sounding like everyday <u>spoken</u> language.
compound word	A word that is made up of two or more other words <u>put together</u>, e.g. "flame-red".
consonants	All the letters in the alphabet that <u>aren't vowels</u>.
contrast	When two things are described in a way which emphasises <u>how different</u> they are. E.g. a poet might contrast two different places or two different people.
dialect	<u>Regional variation</u> of a <u>language</u>. People from different places might use different words or sentence constructions. E.g. In some northern English dialects, people might say "Ey up" instead of "Hello".
empathy	When someone feels like they <u>understand</u> what someone else is experiencing and how they <u>feel</u> about it.
enjambement	When a sentence runs over from <u>one line</u> to the <u>next</u>.
iambic pentameter	This is a form of poetry that doesn't rhyme, but usually has a clear <u>metre</u> of <u>ten syllables</u> — five of them stressed, and five unstressed. The <u>stress</u> falls on <u>every second syllable</u>, e.g. "Co<u>ral</u> is <u>far</u> more <u>red</u> than <u>her</u> lips' <u>red</u>."
imagery	Language that creates a <u>picture in your mind</u>.
irony	When <u>words</u> are used in a <u>sarcastic</u> or <u>comic</u> way to <u>imply the opposite</u> of what they normally mean. It can also mean when there is a big difference between <u>what people expect</u> and <u>what actually happens</u>.
language	The <u>choice of words</u> used. The language determines the effect the piece of writing will have on the reader, e.g. it can be emotive or persuasive.
layout	The way a piece of poetry is visually <u>presented</u> to the reader. E.g. line length, whether the poem is broken up into different stanzas, whether lines are arranged regularly or create some kind of visual pattern.
metaphor	A way of describing something by saying that it <u>is something else</u>, to create a vivid image. E.g. "His eyes were deep, black, oily pools."
metre	The arrangement of syllables to create <u>rhythm</u> in a line of poetry.
mood	The <u>feel</u> or <u>atmosphere</u> of a poem, e.g. humorous, threatening, eerie.
mythology	A collection of very old <u>stories</u>, often involving gods and heroes. Different cultures have their own mythologies.
narrator	The <u>voice</u> speaking the words that you're reading. E.g. a poem could be written from the point of view of a young child, which means the young child is the poem's narrator.

Glossary

noun	A word for a <u>place</u>, <u>person</u> or <u>thing</u>, e.g. "tree", "air", "Boris", "London".
onomatopoeia	A word that <u>sounds like</u> the thing it's describing. E.g. "buzz", "crunch", "bang", "pop", "ding".
persona	A <u>fictional character</u> or <u>identity</u> adopted by a poet. Poets often create a persona so they can describe things from a different person's <u>point of view</u>, e.g. a male poet might use a female persona.
personification	A special kind of metaphor where you write about something as if it's a <u>person</u> with thoughts and feelings. E.g. "The sea growled hungrily."
phonetic	When words are <u>spelt</u> as they <u>sound</u> rather than with their usual spelling. It's often used to show that someone's speaking with a certain <u>accent</u>.
rhyme scheme	A regular <u>system</u> of rhyming words in a poem, e.g. in 'The Man He Killed', the 1st line of each verse rhymes with the 3rd, and the 2nd rhymes with the 4th.
rhyming couplet	A pair of lines that are next to each other and whose final words <u>rhyme</u>.
rhythm	When sentences or lines have a <u>regular fixed pattern</u> of syllables.
simile	A way of describing something by <u>comparing</u> it to something else, usually by using the words "like" or "as". E.g. "He was as pale as the moon," or "Her hair was like a bird's nest."
sonnet	A type of poem with <u>fourteen lines</u>, and usually following a <u>clear rhyme pattern</u>. There are different popular patterns for sonnets. They will often have ten syllables a line, and end with a rhyming couplet.
stanza	A <u>group of lines</u> in a poem that often share the same rhythm pattern and have similar line lengths. Stanzas can also be called <u>verses</u>.
stereotype	An inaccurate, <u>generalised</u> view of a particular <u>group of people</u>. E.g. A stereotype of football fans might be that they're all hooligans.
structure	The <u>order</u> and arrangement of a piece of writing. E.g. how the poem begins, develops and ends, whether it uses verses or not, whether it has a particular layout, etc.
syllable	A single <u>unit of sound</u> within a word. E.g. "all" has one syllable, "always" has two and "establishmentarianism" has nine.
symbolism	When an object <u>stands for something else</u>. E.g. a candle might be a symbol of hope, or a dying flower could symbolise the end of a relationship.
syntax	The way a sentence is put together so that it <u>makes sense</u>.
theme	An <u>idea</u> or <u>topic</u> that's important in a piece of writing. E.g. a poem could be based on the theme of friendship.
verb	A word that describes something you <u>do</u>, e.g. "run", "talk", "hope".
vocabulary	All the <u>words</u> used in a piece of writing.
voice	The <u>personality</u> narrating the poem. Poems are usually written either using the poet's voice, as if they're speaking to you <u>directly</u>, or the voice of a <u>character</u>, e.g. an elderly man, or a horse.
vowels	Simple — the letters 'a', 'e', 'i', 'o' and 'u'.

Index

Index

The Publisher would like to thank:

Poets:

Carol Ann Duffy 'Elvis's Twin Sister', 'Anne Hathaway' and 'Salome' from *The World's Wife* (Picador Macmillan, 1999),
© Carol Ann Duffy 1999, reprinted by permission of the publisher, Macmillan, London, UK.
'Education for Leisure' is taken from *Standing Female Nude* by Carol Ann Duffy published by Anvil Press Poetry in 1985.
'Stealing' is taken from *Selling Manhattan* by Carol Ann Duffy published by Anvil Press Poetry in 1987.
'Havisham' and 'Before You Were Mine' are taken from *Mean Time* by Carol Ann Duffy published by Anvil Press Poetry in 1993.
'We Remember Your Childhood Well' is taken from *The Other Country* by Carol Ann Duffy published by Anvil Press Poetry in 1990.

Simon Armitage 'Hitcher', 'Those bastards in their mansions', 'My father thought it bloody queer', 'Mother', 'Kid', 'I've made out
a will' and 'Homecoming' from *Selected Poems* (2001) all reprinted by permission of the publishers, Faber & Faber Ltd.
 'November', Simon Armitage *ZOOM!* (Bloodaxe Books, 1989)

William Butler Yeats 'The Song of the Old Mother' published by permission of A.P. Watt Ltd. on behalf of Michael B. Yeats

Image sources:

Image of Carol Ann Duffy © Anvil Press

Images of Ben Jonson, William Wordsworth, William Blake, John Clare, Thomas Hardy, Walt Whitman,
Robert Browning, Alfred Lord Tennyson and Oliver Goldsmith © Mary Evans Picture Library

Images of William Butler Yeats and Gerard Manley Hopkins © National Portrait Gallery, London

Image of William Shakespeare © Royal Shakespeare Company

Image of Simon Armitage © www.roderickfield.com

*Every effort has been made to locate copyright holders and obtain permission to reproduce poems and images.
For those poems and images where it has been difficult to trace the originator of the work, we would be grateful
for information. If any copyright holder would like us to make an amendment to the acknowledgements, please
notify us and we will gladly update the book at the next reprint. Thank you.*